At the age of ___
with 'social anxiety ___
carry on working. As t___

housebound as a result of his illness and as such lost touch with many parts of life which although enjoyable are often taken for granted. Simple pleasures such as buying a nice sandwich from a local café or going out for a meal became impossible for him to do.

As a result of this, and because of his love of food and cooking, he eventually took to trying to recreate many of his favourite shop-bought foods at home. 'If I can't go to McDonalds, I'll make my own,' was his philosophy. Over a period of five years or more, he tested and tweaked many, many recipes, his new hobby quickly building into an obsession.

In 2010, Kenny decided to publish some selected recipes in his first book, *The Takeaway Secret*. It became an instant bestseller, following word-of-mouth recommendations on the internet.

With huge support and encouragement from readers, his confidence has grown, along with his food obsession. As a result Kenny once more ventured out into the world. researching and learning about the historic links between street food and local people and the recent upsurge in the modern, exciting and vibrant street food culture. His next book, *The Street Food Secret*, followed in 2017, closely followed by *The American Diner Secret* in 2019.

ALSO BY KENNY MCGOVERN

The Takeaway Secret

The American Takeaway Secret

More Takeaway Secrets

The Street Food Secret

The Takeaway Secret (2nd edition)

The American Diner Secret

THE INDIAN TAKEAWAY SECRET

*How to Cook Your Favourite
Indian Dishes at Home*

Kenny McGovern

A HOW TO BOOK

ROBINSON

ROBINSON

First published in Great Britain in 2021 by Robinson

1 3 5 7 9 10 8 6 4 2

Copyright © Kenny McGovern, 2021

The moral right of the author has been asserted.

All rights reserved.
No part of this publication may be reproduced, stored in a retrieval system,
or transmitted, in any form, or by any means, without the prior permission in
writing of the publisher, nor be otherwise circulated in any form of binding or
cover other than that in which it is published and without a similar condition
including this condition being imposed on the subsequent purchaser.

A CIP catalogue record for this book
is available from the British Library.

ISBN: 978-1-47214-541-3

Typeset in New Caledonia by Hewer Text UK Ltd, Edinburgh
Printed and bound in Great Britain by Clays Ltd, Elcograf S.p.A.

Papers used by Robinson are from well-managed forests and other responsible sources.

MIX
Paper from
responsible sources
FSC® C104740

Robinson
An imprint of
Little, Brown Book Group
Carmelite House
50 Victoria Embankment
London EC4Y 0DZ

An Hachette UK Company
www.hachette.co.uk

www.littlebrown.co.uk

How To Books are published by Robinson, an imprint of Little, Brown Book
Group. We welcome proposals from authors who have first-hand experience
of their subjects. Please set out the aims of your book, its target market
and its suggested contents in an email to howto@littlebrown.co.uk

NOTES ON THE RECIPES

All eggs used in the book are large eggs.

All milk used in the book is whole milk/full-fat milk.

When purchasing spices, try not to buy more than you need for the foreseeable future – fresh spices will add great flavour to your dishes while older spices will lose some of their flavour and aroma over time.

Oven temperatures relate to standard oven temperatures – for fan-assisted ovens, cooking time should be reduced slightly, or cooking temperature lowered by 20°C.

Recipes may be scaled up or down as desired, providing quantity ratios remain consistent. However, when cooking curry sauces proper reduction of the sauce is desired and so cooking one portion at a time is advised.

ACKNOWLEDGEMENTS

This book exists thanks to the invention and hard work of countless takeaway and restaurant chefs who have created such a wide variety of dishes over the years. With every curry dish ordered, a new flavour or aroma is discovered and their creativity and passion for the dishes they serve is to be admired. The dishes included in this book can of course be found at most (if not all) Indian restaurants, but I've been influenced mostly by my own experiences from various curry houses, including Kebab City, Lassani, The Ashoka, and The Anarkali in Glasgow, as well as Ashiq's, Masala Grill and The Viceroy in Dunfermline. Special mention goes to Ohms from The Viceroy restaurant in particular for his encouragement, cooking tips and advice. Credit also goes to the long list of takeaway and fast food fans online who share my passion for recreating these dishes and more besides. Their advice and knowledge has been ever valuable, and I've been lucky enough to make some good friends online amongst a community of encouraging and delightful people, including Dan Toombs (The Curry Guy), Andy Cheung, Alex Wilkie, Frank Mooney, Ohms, Mistrychef,

SavvytheNerd, Lou, Kirsty Bowker, Louise Boyle, Phil H, Sarah-Louise Kelly and many more.

Thanks and appreciation as always go to my family and friends for their encouragement and for helping me in taste-testing various recipes – Margaret, Frank, Stephen, Deborah, Mike, Roisin, Christy, Ian, Alexx, Rebecca, Adele, Audrey, John, Sam, Larraine – not forgetting Phoebe, almost certainly my youngest enthusiastic taste-tester so far. Thanks too to all the staff at Little, Brown for allowing me to share my food obsessions through these books and for being ever encouraging and open to new ideas. Last, but certainly not least, my huge thanks to you for picking up this book. I hope that when you try my recipes you'll be pleased with the results.

CONTENTS

INTRODUCTION

Indian cooking is perhaps the greatest proof that variety really is the spice of life. The vast use of different herbs and spices results in dishes that are packed full of flavour. Often misunderstood by those who are slightly fearful of the hotter dishes available, Indian cooking uses a wide variety of aromatic ingredients to add depth of flavour to every dish and these aromatics and spices are not necessarily all hot.

Of course, as with many cuisines, the dishes popularised around the world vary from country to country. Scotland's large Indian and Pakistani communities have influenced curry houses around the country, in some cases laying claim to the very invention of some of the UK's most popular dishes, including Chicken Tikka Masala, Chicken Chasni, and many others. Nowadays, many Indian restaurants offer real fusion food – dishes such as Haggis Pakora – that celebrate both India and Scotland. This marriage of cultures and cuisines is just one of the many benefits of the multicultural world we live in.

My obsession with recreating takeaway and fast food dishes over the years has led me to become more experienced with spices and the ways in which they can be used across various dishes. This book includes recipes for dishes which will be very familiar to British curry fans – including classics like Vegetable Pakoras and Pink Pakora Sauce, Spiced Onions and more – as well as some more traditional or street food-style Indian dishes such as Disco Fry Egg, Akoori and Aloo Sabzi. If you're a fan of the Indian food you've known and enjoyed in the UK, I hope you'll find it both interesting and rewarding to explore some less familiar dishes as well.

Indian takeaway and restaurant chefs work tirelessly to prepare fresh ingredients and all manner of spicy, sweet, savoury and sour curry sauces for you to enjoy. As we learn more about how to recreate these dishes at home, let's not forget our local restaurant chefs. A takeaway is always a treat and, even in the name of research, the curry house chefs in your area both deserve and will welcome your custom, so don't be a stranger to them. Chances are, with every order you place and every meal you enjoy, you'll be ever more inspired to take to the kitchen and have a go.

Happy cooking!

Indian restaurant and takeaway dishes are markedly different from traditional homecooked Indian dishes. You'll find a note at the start of each recipe indicating the cooking style used.

Weight	
METRIC	IMPERIAL
25g	1oz
50g	2oz
75g	3oz
100g	4oz
150g	5oz
175g	6oz
200g	7oz
225g	8oz
250g	9oz
300g	10oz
350g	12oz
400g	14oz
450g	1lb

Measurements	
METRIC	IMPERIAL
5cm	2in
10cm	4in
13cm	5in
15cm	6in
18cm	7in
20cm	8in
25cm	10in
30cm	12in

Liquids		
METRIC	IMPERIAL	US CUP
5ml	1 tsp	1 tsp
15ml	1 tbsp	1 tbsp
50ml	2fl oz	3 tbsp
60ml	2½fl oz	¼ cup
75ml	3fl oz	⅓ cup
100ml	4fl oz	scant ½ cup
125ml	4½ oz	½ cup
150ml	5fl oz	⅔ cup
200ml	7fl oz	scant 1 cup
250ml	9fl oz	1 cup
300ml	½ pint	1¼ cups
350ml	12fl oz	1⅓ cups
400ml	¾ pint	1¾ cups
500ml	17fl oz	2 cups
600ml	1 pint	2½ cups

STORE CUPBOARD INGREDIENTS

If you're new to Indian cooking, the vast array of spices and ingredients can appear daunting at first. However, just like salt and pepper, with a little experience and experimentation you'll soon become comfortable and used to the different flavours and aromas each ingredient can bring. Listed below are some of the most common store cupboard ingredients which are used regularly in Indian restaurants and home kitchens and are good to have in stock.

Bay Leaves – Indian bay leaves impart aromatic flavours of cinnamon and cloves to flavoured oil or tarkas, though regular bay leaves can be substituted if you can't source Indian bay leaves.

Black Peppercorns – Can be used whole in flavoured oil, or crushed or ground to add a different kind of heat to spicy dishes.

Beetroot Powder – Used to add a vibrant red colour to Spiced Onions (page 197) and curry dishes. I prefer to use this natural ingredient over artificial food colourings.

Chaat Masala – A spice blend including black salt and mango powder among other ingredients. This spice is used to season chaat (snack-type) dishes and salads and has a slightly sweet and acidic flavour.

Chapati Flour (also known as Atta) – A wholemeal wheat flour used to make chapatis, parathas, puri breads and more.

Chickpeas (tinned) – Convenient pre-cooked chickpeas are a great store cupboard ingredient and can be added to curry dishes or chaat snacks.

Chilli Powder – Used to add heat and rich colour to various dishes. Kashmiri red chilli powder is typically a little milder than others and is ideal when you want to add colour without adding too much heat to a dish. Mild, hot or extra hot chilli powder will add vibrant heat to curry dishes.

Cinnamon Sticks/Cassia Bark – True cinnamon (also known as Ceylon cinnamon) is more expensive than cassia (often called Chinese cinnamon), hence many restaurants (and indeed supermarkets) rely on cassia bark to do the same job. Used to flavour oils, the aromatic flavour profile of cinnamon is slightly sweet and citrusy.

Cloves – Add warmth and spice to various dishes including flavoured oils and Masala Chai (spiced tea).

Coriander Seeds and Coriander Powder – Add a warm-spicy and slightly citrusy flavour to dishes.

Creamed Coconut, Coconut Flour and Desiccated Coconut – Used in curry sauces, creamed coconut block will add a smooth, rich finish to your dishes. Both creamed coconut and coconut flour are used in various korma-style sauces. Desiccated coconut is also used in some dishes to add texture and a slight sweetness to the dish.

Cumin Seeds and Cumin Powder – Add a warm, earthy flavour to various dishes and are widely used in tarkas or flavoured oils.

Dates – These sweet and chewy dried fruits are utterly delicious and have a caramel and toffee-like flavour. Added to sour tamarind in Date & Tamarind Chutney (page 209), the resultant flavour is fantastically indulgent and matches perfectly with fried foods.

Dried Red Chillies – Used to add a little heat and a lot of colour to various dishes and tarkas.

Fenugreek – Dried fenugreek leaves (also known as methi or quasoori methi) are widely used in Indian restaurant cooking and add a delicious savoury flavour to curry sauces.

Garam Masala – Typically whole garam masala (a blend of coriander seeds, cumin seeds, cassia, bay leaf, etc.) is used at the start of the cooking process to flavour oils, while the roasted ground spices turned into garam masala powder are added more often towards the end of cooking, although in Indian restaurant-style cooking the process is so quick that the beginning is almost the end! Garam masala is aromatic, spicy and sweet.

Ghee – A form of clarified butter, ghee is rich and indulgent and can be used both as a cooking fat or as an addition to cooked chapatis, naan breads, etc. It has a nutty aroma and is extremely moreish.

Gram Flour (chickpea flour) – Also known as besan, gram flour is an essential ingredient for creating a flavourful, crispy coating in pakora dishes.

Lemon Dressing – While purists will of course argue that fresh lemon juice is best, many Indian restaurant chefs use lemon dressing as an alternative. Lemon dressing is typically made using lemon concentrate and citric acid. It's inexpensive, has a long shelf life and adds a deliciously sour and tangy finish to curry dishes and salads or chaats.

Lentils – Used in various dal dishes as well as being a key ingredient in Dansak (page 97).

Mango Chutney – As well as being utterly delicious scooped up with crispy poppadoms, mango chutney is used in various Indian restaurant curry dishes to add a sweet and sour flavour. I like the Geeta's brand.

Mint Sauce – Used in tikka marinades and an essential ingredient in Spiced Onions (page 197) and Pink Pakora Sauce (page 212).

Mustard Seeds – Used to flavour oil or tarkas, mustard seeds will pop excitedly in hot oil and add warmth and spice.

Nigella Seeds – Also known as kalonji seeds or black onion seeds, these can be added to naan breads and have a slightly bitter, smoky and caramelised onion flavour.

Nylon Sev – These thin, crispy gram flour noodles are a delicious snack and are ideal for topping chaat and salad dishes.

Poppadoms (ready to fry) – A perfect store cupboard essential, these poppadoms have a long shelf life and can be cooked in hot oil in just a few seconds, allowing you to enjoy fresh and crispy poppadoms with your favourite curry dishes any time you choose.

Rice – Although 'instant' rice pouches are widely available and can be very convenient, it's worth investing in good quality basmati rice to accompany your curry dishes. Use my method on page 186 to cook foolproof Plain Basmati Rice.

Rice Flour – Combined with gram flour, rice flour adds a delicious light crispness to pakoras and can also be used to make Instant Dosas (page 150).

Tamarind Block – Another excellent long-life store cupboard ingredient, dried tamarind block can be soaked in hot water before pressing through a sieve to produce tamarind paste whenever you may require it. Tamarind has a sweet and sour flavour.

Tomato Purée, Tomato Passata and Tomato Ketchup – Sweet and rich, tomatoes in various forms are widely used in Indian restaurant cooking. Ketchup is the building block for perfect Spiced Onions (page 197) and is widely added to curry sauces such as Patia (page 99).

Turmeric Powder – Adds colour and a slightly bitter and pungent flavour to dishes, and is very good for your health.

Vegetable Oil – Used in large quantities, of course, for Curry Broth (pages 68 and 72) and for frying pakoras, bhajis and poppadoms. If you're conscious of consuming too much oil, use the amount required in each recipe regardless – this will ensure the spices are cooked out as they should be and any excess oil can easily be spooned off after cooking and discarded (or better still, stored for future use in fried rice dishes or curry broth).

FRESH INGREDIENTS

Coriander Leaves – Add a fresh citrus finish to all manner of curry dishes, as well as an attractive decorative effect. A small minority of people may have an unfortunate genetic dislike of fresh coriander and find it leaves a soapy taste in the mouth. If you're not one of those people, count yourself lucky and indulge in fresh coriander often!

Lemons – Preferred by many over lemon dressing, fresh lemon juice is acidic and cuts through fatty foods, hence lemon slices are often served with fried foods such as pakoras (or fish and chips!).

Milk – Used in Lassi (page 218), milk is the perfect way to cool down the palate when indulging in a particularly hot dish. It is also used to make Paneer Cheese (page 233) and to thin out Pink Pakora Sauce (page 212).

Onions – You simply can't begin to recreate Indian restaurant food without onions, and you'll need a lot of them! They are the primary ingredient in Curry Broth (pages 68 and 72), as well as being used in all manner of side dishes such as Spiced Onions (page 197) and Vegetable Pakoras (page 18).

Spinach Leaves – Added to curry dishes, spinach leaves will quickly wilt and reduce almost like magic – if you think you've added too much spinach to your dish, let it cook down for just a minute and you'll find it almost disappears! Spinach is also a common ingredient in Vegetable Pakoras (page 18).

Spring Onions – Some of the hotter curry dishes you'll find in this book such as South Indian Garlic Chilli (page 108) and Sharabi (page 117) are often finished with thinly sliced spring onions as well as the more traditional fresh coriander leaves.

Yogurt – Adding creamy yogurt to a particularly spicy dish is a great way to mellow the heat (I prefer to add yogurt at the end, after switching off the heat, as it can easily split if cooked in the sauce). Yogurt is also used widely in Indian restaurants to make dips, including Mint Sauce (page 214) and Pink Pakora Sauce (page 212).

EQUIPMENT

In order to authentically recreate Indian takeaway food at home, there are various pieces of equipment and utensils that can help us achieve our goals. While not essential, if you're serious about all things curry, you'll most certainly be interested in adding these items to your kitchen.

Aluminium Frying Pan (22cm) – Used widely in the catering industry, aluminium pans can reach the required temperature quickly and allow sauces to catch a little on the surface of the pan. This might sound undesirable, but this caramelisation actually adds greatly to the flavour of the curry. When serving up your curry, be sure not to miss any of those flavours by scraping every possible drop of sauce from your cooking pan to your serving plate.

Foil Trays and Containers (or an eco-friendly reusable alternative) – If you're as obsessed with recreating takeaway food as I am, you'll want to invest in foil containers to add authenticity to your exploits. As well as adding a takeaway restaurant

13

feel to proceedings, they're also very useful for keeping cooked dishes warm, allowing you time to prepare accompanying dishes before serving.

Pestle and Mortar – Used to make small amounts of various chutneys and pastes. Unless you are making large amounts of chutneys or pastes, a blender will often struggle and you'll find yourself continually having to stop and scrape the ingredients down from the side of the bowl. Although a little more time-consuming to use, a good quality, heavy granite pestle and mortar will often do a much better job, as well as offering a more hands-on cooking experience.

Spice Box – These stainless steel tins are ideal for storing regularly used spices (my own box contains cumin powder, coriander powder, garam masala, turmeric, Kashmiri red chilli powder, dried fenugreek leaves and sea salt). Spice boxes make life immeasurably easier when it comes to Indian cooking, and avoid the need to open and close various packets of spices each time.

Stick Blender – Used to blend Curry Broth (pages 68 and 72) until smooth. An essential item!

Stock Pot – If you are making a full batch of Curry Broth (page 68), a large stock pot is also essential.

Tandoor Oven – Of course, the unique flavour a tandoor oven imparts to food is part of the restaurant experience, adding smoke and char to tikka dishes and naan breads. If you're lucky enough to own one, consider me extremely jealous!

Tava or Chapati Pan – Choose either a heavy cast-iron tava or a good quality non-stick chapati pan. These pans are ideal for preparing chapati breads, paratha breads and dosas.

STARTERS AND APPETISERS

While the main course curry dishes are the stars of the show, the perfect Indian restaurant experience starts with light and crispy pakoras, onion bhajis, meat kebabs and more. These flavourful starter dishes are an introduction to, and indication of, the delights that lie ahead.

As a general rule, I like to fry pakoras twice. As well as adding a more pronounced flavour and extra crunch to the finished pakoras, it also makes life easier because the pakoras themselves can be prepared ahead of time (even the day before), the washing up taken care of and the main curry dishes prepared. With a final flash-fry in hot oil, you can serve the pakoras up in a matter of minutes!

VEGETABLE PAKORAS (INDIAN RESTAURANT STYLE)

If you like your vegetable pakoras particularly spicy, you can add 1–2 fresh green finger chillies, thinly sliced, to the pakora mix, or serve with Red Chilli Sauce (page 211).

Serves 6 (Makes about 24 small pakoras)

- 3 medium onions, thinly sliced (about 200g peeled weight)
- 3 small new potatoes, peeled and finely chopped (about 100g peeled weight)
- 1 handful baby spinach leaves, finely chopped
- 2 teaspoons thinly sliced fresh coriander stems (optional)
- Pinch of cumin seeds
- ¼ teaspoon cumin powder
- Pinch of coriander seeds
- ¼ teaspoon coriander powder
- ½ teaspoon garam masala
- ¼ teaspoon turmeric
- ¼ teaspoon mild red chilli powder
- ½ teaspoon dried fenugreek leaves (methi)
- ¼ teaspoon Garlic Ginger Paste (page 228)
- ¼ teaspoon sea salt, plus extra to serve
- 1 teaspoon fresh lemon juice or lemon dressing
- Vegetable oil for deep-frying
- 2–3 tablespoons water

About 100g gram flour (chickpea flour)
1–2 tablespoons rice flour

To serve
Onion & Coriander Salad (page 201) (optional)
Pink Pakora Sauce (page 212)

- Put the sliced onions, chopped potatoes, chopped spinach leaves, sliced coriander stems (if desired), cumin seeds, cumin powder, coriander seeds, coriander powder, garam masala, turmeric, mild red chilli powder, dried fenugreek leaves, garlic ginger paste, sea salt and fresh lemon juice or lemon dressing in a large bowl. Mix thoroughly and set aside for 1 hour. During this time, the salt will draw water from the vegetables, reducing the amount of added water required; this increases the flavour of the finished pakoras.

- After the pakora mix has rested for around 1 hour, heat the oil for deep-frying to 170°C/340°F. If you're using a deep-fat fryer with a basket, remove the basket before heating the oil (the pakoras would stick to the basket).

- Add 2–3 tablespoons of water to the prepared pakora mix then slowly add the gram flour and rice flour, mixing well and adding a little more water and flour as necessary until the pakora mix has a slightly thick consistency and slides slowly off the back of a spoon. Using two forks, carefully slide one forkful of pakora mix at a time into the hot oil.

Using a fork increases the amount of rough areas on the batter and results in extra-crispy pakoras.

- Fry the pakoras in batches (I usually fry 8 or 9 at a time) for 3–4 minutes, turning them occasionally, until golden and crisp. Using a slotted spoon, lift the pakoras out and transfer them to a plate. Repeat with the remaining batter. Leave to stand for 5 minutes. Alternatively, let them cool completely and keep covered in the refrigerator for up to 2 days until required.

- To finish the vegetable pakoras, heat the oil for deep-frying to 180°C/350°F. Carefully place the pakoras in the hot oil and fry for 2 minutes until hot and crunchy. Use a slotted spoon to remove the pakoras from the oil and place on a plate lined with kitchen paper to drain off any excess oil.

- Season the pakoras with a little sea salt. Garnish with onion and coriander salad (if desired) and serve with pink pakora sauce.

MUSHROOM PAKORAS (INDIAN RESTAURANT STYLE)

Serves 1–2 (Makes 8–10 pakoras)

5 tablespoons gram flour (chickpea flour)
¼ teaspoon cumin powder
¼ teaspoon coriander powder
¼ teaspoon garam masala
½ teaspoon dried fenugreek leaves (methi)
Pinch of turmeric
¼ teaspoon Kashmiri red chilli powder
½ teaspoon sea salt, plus extra to serve
60–75ml cold water
4–5 large button mushrooms, halved
Vegetable oil for deep-frying

To serve
Onion & Coriander Salad (page 201) (optional)
Pink Pakora Sauce (page 212)

- Put the gram flour, cumin powder, coriander powder, garam masala, dried fenugreek, turmeric, red chilli powder and sea salt in a large bowl. Mix well. Slowly add the water (you may not need it all), whisking until you have a smooth, slightly thick batter. The consistency should be similar to that of double cream.

- Heat the oil for deep-frying to 180°C/350°F. If you're using a deep-fat fryer with a basket, remove the basket before heating the oil (the pakoras would stick to the basket).

- Two small wooden skewers are useful at this stage, to work with the mushrooms without getting your hands coated in pakora batter. Add the mushrooms to the batter. To transfer the mushrooms to the oil, pierce each mushroom with a skewer and use the other skewer to encourage the battered mushroom carefully into the hot oil. Repeat until as many mushrooms as will fit comfortably are added to the hot oil (cook the mushroom pakoras in two batches if necessary).

- Fry the mushroom pakoras for 2–3 minutes – be careful, they will spit a little as the water in the mushrooms comes out. Using a slotted spoon, lift the pakoras out and transfer to a plate. Repeat with the remaining mushroom pieces. Leave to stand for 5 minutes. Alternatively, let them cool completely and keep covered in the refrigerator for up to 2 days until required.

- To finish the mushroom pakoras, heat the oil to 190°C/375°F. Fry the pakoras in batches in the hot oil for 2 minutes, or until golden and crispy.

- Use a slotted spoon to remove the pakoras and place on a plate lined with kitchen paper to drain off any excess oil.

- Season the pakoras with a little sea salt. Garnish with onion and coriander salad (if desired) and serve with pink pakora sauce.

CAULIFLOWER PAKORAS
(TRADITIONAL INDIAN STYLE)

Serves 1–2 (Makes 10–12 pakoras)

250g cauliflower, roughly cut into bite-sized pieces
¼ teaspoon cumin powder
¼ teaspoon coriander powder
¼ teaspoon garam masala
Pinch of turmeric
Pinch of asafoetida
½ teaspoon Kashmiri red chilli powder
Pinch of ajwain (carom seeds) (optional)
¼ teaspoon sea salt, plus extra to serve
3–4 tablespoons gram flour (chickpea flour)
1–2 tablespoons rice flour
3–4 tablespoons cold water
Vegetable oil for deep-frying

To serve
Onion & Coriander Salad (page 201) (optional)
Date & Tamarind Chutney (page 209)

- Bring a pan of salted water to the boil. Carefully add the cauliflower pieces and boil for 2 minutes. Drain the water, rinse the cauliflower briefly in cold water, drain again and set aside in a bowl.

- To the bowl of cauliflower, add the cumin powder, coriander powder, garam masala, turmeric, asafoetida, Kashmiri red chilli powder, ajwain/carom seeds (if desired) and sea salt. Mix well and set aside for 10 minutes.

- Heat the oil for deep-frying to 170°C/340°F. If you're using a deep-fat fryer with a basket, remove the basket before heating the oil (the pakoras would stick to the basket).

- Add the gram flour, rice flour and water to the spiced cauliflower pieces and gently mix until the flour and water forms a sticky coating. Carefully place some of the coated cauliflower pieces in the hot oil and fry for 4–6 minutes, or until golden and crisp. Using a slotted spoon, lift the pakoras out and transfer to a plate. Repeat with the remaining cauliflower pieces. Leave to stand for 5 minutes. Alternatively, let them cool completely and keep covered in the refrigerator for up to 2 days until required.

- To finish the cauliflower pakoras, heat the oil for deep-frying to 180°C/350°F. Fry the pakora pieces in batches in the hot oil for 2 minutes until hot and crunchy. Use a slotted spoon to remove the pakoras from the oil and place on a plate lined with kitchen paper to drain off any excess oil. Repeat with the remaining pakora pieces.

- Season the pakoras with a little sea salt. Garnish with onion and coriander salad (if desired) and serve with date and tamarind chutney.

SWEETCORN PAKORAS (INDIAN RESTAURANT STYLE)

These delicious little nuggets of corn are slightly sweet and spicy, and are equally good hot or at room temperature. If you need to reheat the pakoras, arrange them on a baking tray and reheat in the oven at 180°C/Gas 4 for about 12 minutes.

Serves 2–3 (Makes about 20 pakoras)

- ¼ teaspoon chaat masala
- ½ teaspoon garam masala
- ½ teaspoon cumin seeds
- ¼ teaspoon coriander seeds
- ¼ teaspoon Kashmiri red chilli powder
- ½ teaspoon dried fenugreek leaves (methi)
- Pinch of turmeric
- ¼ teaspoon sea salt
- 325g salt tin sweetcorn (260g drained weight), drained and rinsed
- 1 fresh green chilli, thinly sliced
- 1 spring onion, thinly sliced
- 1 teaspoon Garlic Ginger Paste (page 228)
- Dash of fresh lemon juice or lemon dressing
- Vegetable oil for deep-frying
- 4 tablespoons gram flour (chickpea flour)
- 2 tablespoons rice flour
- Pink Pakora Sauce (page 212) or tomato ketchup, to serve

- Put the chaat masala, garam masala, cumin seeds, coriander seeds, Kashmiri red chilli powder, dried fenugreek leaves, turmeric and sea salt in a bowl. Mix and set aside.

- Put half of the drained sweetcorn in a pestle and mortar and pound to a rough paste – it's not essential to completely purée the corn, just roughly mashed is fine. Tip the roughly mashed sweetcorn into a large bowl. Add the remaining sweetcorn kernels, the prepared spices, green chilli, spring onion, garlic ginger paste and lemon juice. Mix thoroughly and set aside for 20 minutes.

- Heat the oil for deep-frying to about 180°C/350°F. If you're using a deep-fat fryer with a basket, remove the basket before heating the oil (the pakoras would stick to the basket).

- Slowly add the gram flour and rice flour to the pakora mixture, mixing well and adding a little water or more flour as necessary until the pakora mix has a slightly thick consistency and slides slowly off the back of a spoon.

- Cook them in small batches (I managed to fit about 6 pakoras into the oil at one time). Carefully drop the mixture into the hot oil a teaspoonful at a time, using a second teaspoon to help shape the pakora on the spoon, and fry for about 5 minutes, or until the pakoras are crispy and golden. Lift the cooked pakoras out of the oil using a slotted spoon and set aside on a plate in the oven at the lowest available heat to keep warm. Repeat the process until all of the sweetcorn pakoras are cooked.

- Serve the pakoras with pink pakora sauce or tomato ketchup.

CHICKEN PAKORAS (INDIAN RESTAURANT STYLE)

This recipe can be scaled up, providing quantities are increased proportionately. The twice-frying process makes it easy to prepare lots of pakoras the day before, ready to finish and serve to hungry guests the following day.

Serves 1 (Makes 6–8 pakoras)

 1 large skinless, boneless chicken breast fillet (about
   150g), cut into 6–8 long strips
 1 teaspoon Tandoori Paste (page 230)
 ½ teaspoon Garlic Ginger Paste (page 228)
 Dash of fresh lemon juice or lemon dressing
 ¼ teaspoon sea salt, plus extra to serve
 Vegetable oil for deep-frying
 3 tablespoons gram flour (chickpea flour)
 1 tablespoon rice flour
 1 tablespoon cold water

To serve
Onion & Coriander Salad (page 201) (optional)
Pink Pakora Sauce (page 212)

- Put the sliced chicken breast, tandoori paste, garlic ginger paste, lemon juice or dressing and sea salt in a bowl. Mix well, cover and set aside in the refrigerator for 1 hour.

- Heat the oil for deep-frying to 170°C/340°F. If you're using a deep-fat fryer with a basket, remove the basket before heating the oil (the pakoras would stick to the basket).

- Add the gram flour, rice flour and water to the marinated chicken and mix gently until the water and flour forms a sticky coating. Carefully place the chicken pakora pieces into the hot oil and fry for about 4 minutes until the chicken is just cooked through and the batter is golden and crispy. Using a slotted spoon, lift the pakoras out and transfer to a plate. Set aside for 5 minutes. Alternatively, let them cool completely and keep covered in the refrigerator for up to 2 days until required.

- To finish the chicken pakoras, heat the oil for deep-frying to 180°C/350°F. Carefully place the pakoras in the hot oil and fry for about 2 minutes, or until hot and crunchy. Use a slotted spoon to remove the pakoras from the oil and place on a plate lined with kitchen paper to drain off any excess oil.

- Season the pakoras with a little sea salt. Garnish with onion and coriander salad (if desired) and serve with pink pakora sauce.

HAGGIS PAKORAS (INDIAN RESTAURANT STYLE)

If Scotland's Indian cuisine is unique to the country itself, there can surely be no better example of the fusion of both countries and cultures than haggis pakoras.

Serves 2 (Makes 12 haggis pakoras)

4 tablespoons gram flour (chickpea flour)
1 tablespoon rice flour
¼ teaspoon garam masala
¼ teaspoon coriander powder
¼ teaspoon cumin powder
Pinch of turmeric
Pinch of Kashmiri red chilli powder
½ teaspoon dried fenugreek leaves (methi)
½ teaspoon sea salt, plus extra to serve
60–75ml cold water
Vegetable oil for deep-frying
3 slices of haggis, each cut into 4 quarters

To serve
Onion & Coriander Salad (page 201) (optional)
Pink Pakora Sauce (page 212)

- Put the gram flour, rice flour, garam masala, coriander powder, cumin powder, turmeric, Kashmiri red chilli powder, dried fenugreek leaves and sea salt in a large bowl. Mix well.

- Add the water a little at a time (you may not need it all) until you have a smooth, slightly thick batter. The consistency should be similar to that of double cream. If the mix is too thin, add a little more gram flour. If it's too thick, add a little more water.

- Heat the oil for deep-frying to 180°C/350°F. If you're using a deep-fat fryer with a basket, remove the basket before heating the oil (the pakoras would stick to the basket).

- Carefully dip each haggis piece into the batter then into the hot oil. Cook the pakoras in batches (I managed to fit about 6 pakoras into the oil at one time). Fry the haggis pakoras for 3–4 minutes, or until crisp and golden. Remove from the oil using a slotted spoon and set aside on a plate in the oven at the lowest setting to keep warm. Repeat the process until all of the haggis pakoras are cooked.

- Season the pakoras with a little sea salt. Garnish with onion and coriander salad (if desired) and serve with pink pakora sauce.

CHICKEN 65 (INDIAN STREET-FOOD STYLE)

This spicy chicken is the perfect snack, or can be added to curry sauces. Fans of chicken tikka will quickly come to love this dish.

This recipe is easy to scale up – just increase the quantities proportionately.

Serves 1

1 large skinless, boneless chicken breast fillet (about 150g), cut into 5–6 pieces
½ teaspoon Garlic Ginger Paste (page 228)
Pinch of cumin powder
Pinch of coriander powder
Pinch of garam masala
¼ teaspoon paprika
¼ teaspoon Kashmiri red chilli powder
¼ teaspoon beetroot powder (optional, for colour)
½ teaspoon dried fenugreek leaves (methi)
Pinch of sea salt
½ teaspoon distilled white vinegar
1 teaspoon vegetable oil
Vegetable oil for deep-frying
1½ teaspoons plain flour
1½ teaspoons rice flour

To serve
Thinly sliced onions
Fresh coriander leaves, finely chopped
Lemon wedges
Coriander Chutney (page 204)

- Put the chicken pieces in a bowl and add the garlic ginger paste, cumin powder, coriander powder, garam masala, paprika, red chilli powder, beetroot powder (if desired), dried fenugreek leaves, sea salt, white vinegar and vegetable oil. Mix well until all of the chicken pieces are coated. Cover and set aside in the refrigerator for 1 hour.

- Heat the oil for deep-frying to 180°C/350°F. If you're using a deep-fat fryer with a basket, remove the basket before heating the oil (the chicken might stick to the basket).

- Add the plain flour and rice flour to the bowl of marinated chicken and mix well until the chicken pieces are evenly coated. Carefully place the chicken pieces in the hot oil and fry for about 5 minutes, or until the chicken is cooked through and golden. Remove the chicken pieces from the oil with tongs or a slotted spoon, drain off any excess oil on kitchen paper and arrange on a serving tray or on a plate.

- Garnish the Chicken 65 with thinly sliced onions and fresh coriander and serve with lemon wedges and coriander chutney.

AMRITSARI FISH PAKORAS
(TRADITIONAL INDIAN STYLE)

Serves 1–2

2 skinless, boneless cod fillets or any other firm white fish
   (about 275g in total)
1 teaspoon Garlic Ginger Paste (page 228)
½ teaspoon garam masala
½ teaspoon ajwain (carom seeds)
¼ teaspoon Kashmiri red chilli powder
¼ teaspoon turmeric
½ teaspoon dried fenugreek leaves (methi)
¼ teaspoon sea salt
Pinch of ground black pepper
¼ teaspoon beetroot powder (optional, for colour)
1 teaspoon fresh lemon juice or lemon dressing
2–3 tablespoons gram flour (chickpea flour)
1 tablespoon rice flour
1–2 tablespoons water
Vegetable oil for deep-frying
¼ teaspoon chaat masala
Lemon wedges, to serve

- Check the fish for any small bones and cut each fillet into two pieces. Put the fish in a large bowl and add the garlic ginger paste, garam masala, ajwain, red chilli powder, turmeric, dried fenugreek leaves, sea salt and black pepper.

Add the beetroot powder (if desired), then add the fresh lemon juice or lemon dressing, gram flour, rice flour and water and mix well until the fish is evenly coated. Set aside for 15 minutes.

- Heat the oil for deep-frying to 180°C/350°F. If you're using a deep-fat fryer with a basket, remove the basket before heating the oil (the pakoras would stick to the basket).

- Carefully place each marinated piece of fish in the hot oil and fry for 3–4 minutes, or until the fish is cooked through and golden. Remove from the oil with a slotted spoon, drain off any excess oil on kitchen paper and arrange on a serving plate.

- Sprinkle the chaat masala over the fried fish and serve with lemon wedges.

BREAD PAKORAS (TRADITIONAL INDIAN STYLE)

This recipe works best with bread that is slightly dry, making it ideal for using up bread that's not as fresh as it once was. If fresh bread is all you have, leave the slices of bread on the work surface for a couple of hours before cooking.

Serves 1–2 (Makes 4 pakoras)

50g gram flour (chickpea flour)
1 tablespoon rice flour
½ teaspoon cumin seeds
¼ teaspoon ajwain (carom seeds)
¼ teaspoon garam masala
¼ teaspoon Kashmiri red chilli powder
¼ teaspoon turmeric
¼ teaspoon sea salt, plus extra to serve
1 small handful fresh coriander, finely chopped
125ml cold water
2 bread slices
Vegetable oil for deep-frying
Coriander Chutney (page 204) or Date & Tamarind
    Chutney (page 209), to serve

- Put the gram flour, rice flour, cumin seeds, ajwain, garam masala, red chilli powder, turmeric, sea salt and fresh coriander in a large bowl. Mix briefly and slowly add water until the batter has the consistency of single cream.

- Cut the crusts off each bread slice and cut each slice into two equal pieces.

- Heat the oil for deep-frying to 160°C/320°F. If you're using a deep-fat fryer with a basket, remove the basket before heating the oil (the pakoras would stick to the basket).

- Dip each piece of bread into the prepared batter and place it carefully into the hot oil. Fry the bread pakoras for 4–5 minutes, or until crispy and golden. Remove from the oil with a slotted spoon, drain off any excess oil on kitchen paper and arrange on a serving plate, seasoning them with a little sea salt.

- Serve the bread pakoras with coriander chutney or date and tamarind chutney.

ONION BHAJIS (INDIAN RESTAURANT STYLE)

Crispy, spicy and very moreish, these bhajis are the perfect
starter or accompaniment to any curry dish.

Serves 2 (Makes 6 bhajis)

 1 medium-large onion (about 190g peeled weight), halved
   and sliced
 ½ teaspoon Garlic Ginger Paste (page 228)
 1 teaspoon coriander seeds
 ½ teaspoon cumin powder
 ½ teaspoon garam masala
 ½ teaspoon Kashmiri red chilli powder
 ¼ teaspoon turmeric
 ½ teaspoon dried fenugreek leaves (methi)
 ½ teaspoon sea salt, plus extra to serve
 Pinch of bicarbonate of soda
 1 small handful fresh coriander leaves, finely chopped
 1 teaspoon fresh lemon juice or lemon dressing
 Vegetable oil for deep-frying
 50–75g gram flour (chickpea flour)
 1 tablespoon rice flour
 1–2 tablespoons water
 Pink Pakora Sauce (page 212), to serve

- Put the sliced onion, garlic ginger paste, coriander seeds,
  cumin powder, garam masala, red chilli powder, turmeric,

dried fenugreek leaves, sea salt, bicarbonate of soda, fresh coriander leaves and fresh lemon juice or lemon dressing in a large bowl. Mix well and set aside for 1 hour.

- Heat the oil for deep-frying to about 160°C/320°F. If you're using a deep-fat fryer with a basket, remove the basket before heating the oil (the bhajis would stick to the basket).

- Add 50g of the gram flour and all the rice flour to the onion mixture and mix thoroughly, adding a little of the water until the mixture thickens slightly and slides slowly off a spoon (add the remaining gram flour if needed). Using two spoons, carefully add the bhaji mix to the hot oil, 1 heaped tablespoon at a time (the mix should be enough for 6 bhajis). Fry the bhajis for about 5 minutes, turning them occasionally until just beginning to colour. Use a slotted spoon to remove the bhajis from the oil and set aside on a plate to cool completely. At this stage the bhajis can be finished immediately, or covered and set aside in the refrigerator for up to 24 hours.

- To finish the bhajis, heat the oil for deep-frying to about 180°C/350°F. Carefully place the bhajis in the hot oil and fry for about 2 minutes until heated through, golden and crispy. Remove from the oil with a slotted spoon, and place on a plate lined with kitchen paper to drain off excess oil.

- Season the bhajis with a little sea salt and serve with pink pakora sauce.

ALOO TIKKI (INDIAN RESTAURANT STYLE)

A popular north Indian snack of spiced, crisp and tasty potato patties.

Serves 2 (Makes 4 patties)

3 floury potatoes (Maris Piper or King Edward are good), peeled and halved
Pinch of cumin powder
Pinch of coriander powder
Pinch of garam masala
Pinch of turmeric
Pinch of Kashmiri red chilli powder
Pinch of garlic powder
Pinch of ginger powder
½ teaspoon sea salt, plus extra to serve
1 fresh green finger chilli pepper, thinly sliced
1 small handful fresh coriander leaves, finely chopped
1 egg
6 tablespoons breadcrumbs
Vegetable oil for deep-frying
Onion & Coriander Salad (page 201), to serve

• Add the peeled and halved potatoes to a pan, cover with water, add a pinch of salt and bring to the boil. Cook for 10–15 minutes or until the potatoes are just soft.

- Drain the potatoes and return them to the pan.

- Add the cumin powder, coriander powder, garam masala, turmeric, red chilli powder, garlic powder, ginger powder, sea salt, fresh green chilli and fresh coriander. Mash and mix well until all of the ingredients are evenly combined. Allow the mix to cool, then form into 4 equal-sized patties.

- Whisk the egg in a bowl and spread out the breadcrumbs on a plate. Carefully dip the potato patties first into the beaten egg and then into the breadcrumbs. Arrange the breaded patties on a plate, cover and refrigerate for 1–2 hours or overnight. This will help the coating stick to the patties when fried.

- Heat the oil for deep-frying to 180°C/350°F. If you're using a deep-fat fryer with a basket, remove the basket before heating the oil (the patties would stick to the basket).

- Carefully place the potato patties in the hot oil and fry for 3–4 minutes, or until golden and crisp. Remove the aloo tikki from the oil using a slotted spoon, place on a plate lined with kitchen paper to drain off any excess oil then arrange on a serving tray or plate. Season the aloo tikki with a little sea salt and serve with onion and coriander salad.

VEGETABLE SAMOSAS (INDIAN RESTAURANT STYLE)

Frozen samosa wrappers (usually called 'pads') can be found in Asian supermarkets or online. Alternatively, filo pastry sheets or spring roll wrappers cut into two strips will provide equally good results.

Serves 4 (Makes 8–12 samosas)

1 teaspoon sea salt
¼ teaspoon cumin powder
¼ teaspoon cumin seeds
¼ teaspoon coriander powder
1 teaspoon garam masala
¼ teaspoon Kashmiri red chilli powder
Pinch of turmeric
4–6 new potatoes (275–300g)
1 tablespoon vegetable oil
1 small onion, finely chopped
1 teaspoon Garlic Ginger Paste (page 228)
1 fresh green finger chilli, thinly sliced
75g frozen green peas
2 teaspoons fresh lemon juice or lemon dressing
1 tablespoon plain flour mixed with 2 tablespoons water
8–12 frozen samosa pads
Vegetable oil for deep-frying

- Put the sea salt, cumin powder, cumin seeds, coriander powder, garam masala, red chilli powder and turmeric in a small bowl. Mix well and set aside.

- Fill a large pan with water, then add a pinch of salt and the new potatoes. Bring to the boil and simmer for about 12 minutes, or until the potatoes are almost completely soft. Drain and set aside to cool. Once cool enough to handle, peel the potatoes and cut them into small dice.

- Heat the tablespoon of vegetable oil in a curry pan or frying pan over a medium heat. Add the chopped onion and stir-fry for 5–6 minutes until softened, then add the garlic ginger paste and green chilli and cook for a further 1 minute.

- Add the frozen peas and the cooked potatoes and mix well. Add the prepared spice mix along with a splash of water and mix thoroughly. Finish with fresh lemon juice or lemon dressing, mix once more and set aside to cool completely. Refrigerate the mix for about 1 hour. Meanwhile, defrost the samosa pads according to the packet instructions.

- Add a tablespoon (or as much as you can comfortably fit) of the filling mixture to each samosa pad and wrap according to the packet instructions, using the prepared flour and water mix as a glue to seal each samosa. The samosas can now be frozen for future use if desired (many people prefer to freeze samosas briefly, even if using the same day, as it helps ensure the filling won't escape from your samosas during frying).

- To cook the samosas, heat the oil for deep-frying to about 180°C/350°F.

- If you're using a deep-fat fryer with a basket, remove the basket before heating the oil (the samosas would stick to the basket).

- Carefully place the samosas in the hot oil and fry for 3–4 minutes, or until golden and crispy. Remove from the oil with a slotted spoon, place on a plate lined with kitchen paper to drain off any excess oil and serve with your favourite chutneys.

LAMB SAMOSAS (INDIAN RESTAURANT STYLE)

Lamb samosas are a great way to use up leftover Keema (page 124). They're also so delicious that it's worth making a batch intended exclusively for samosas! You'll need a generous tablespoon of keema mattar filling and one samosa pad for each samosa. Alternatively, filo pastry sheets or spring roll wrappers cut into two strips will provide equally good results.

Serves 8–10 (Makes about 40 samosas if using 1 full batch of Keema Mattar)

  1 fresh batch Keema Mattar, cooled (or leftovers) (page 124)
  1 pack frozen samosa pads (defrosted according to the packet instructions)
  2 tablespoons plain flour mixed with 4 tablespoons water
  Vegetable oil for deep-frying

• Add a tablespoon (or as much as you can comfortably fit) of keema mattar to each samosa pad and wrap according to the packet instructions, using the prepared flour and water mix as a glue to seal each samosa. The samosas can now be frozen for future use if desired (many people prefer to freeze samosas briefly, even if using the same day, as it helps ensure the filling won't escape from your samosas during frying).

- To cook the samosas, heat the oil for deep-frying to about 180°C/350°F. If you're using a deep-fat fryer with a basket, remove the basket before heating the oil (the samosas would stick to the basket).

- Carefully place the lamb samosas in the hot oil and fry for 3–4 minutes or until golden and crispy. Remove from the oil with a slotted spoon, place on a plate lined with kitchen paper to drain off any excess oil and serve with your favourite chutneys.

SHORE–E–MURGH (INDIAN RESTAURANT STYLE)

Deliciously spiced chicken wings.

Serves 4 (Makes about 20 wings)

1 generous tablespoon Tandoori Paste (page 230)
6 tablespoons natural yogurt
1 tablespoon fresh lemon juice or lemon dressing
1 teaspoon Garlic Ginger Paste (page 228)
½ teaspoon garam masala
Pinch of paprika
Pinch of turmeric
½ teaspoon Kashmiri red chilli powder
½ teaspoon dried fenugreek leaves (methi)
1 teaspoon sea salt
1kg chicken wings, wingtip removed and wings cut into
    two parts (drumettes and wingettes/flats)
Onion & Coriander Salad (page 201), to serve

- Put the tandoori paste, natural yogurt, fresh lemon juice or lemon dressing, garlic ginger paste, garam masala, paprika, turmeric, red chilli powder, dried fenugreek leaves and sea salt in a large bowl. Mix well. Add the prepared wings, mix thoroughly until evenly coated, cover and set aside in the refrigerator for 2 hours.

- Preheat the oven to 200°C/Gas 6 and line a baking tray with foil. Remove the wings from the marinade, wiping off any excess. Place a wire rack over the lined baking tray, brush it lightly with a little vegetable oil then arrange the wings on the rack. Bake the wings for about 40 minutes until cooked through. Serve with onion and coriander salad.

TANDOORI CHICKEN STARTER (ON THE BONE) (INDIAN RESTAURANT STYLE)

Serves 1–2

2 bone-in, skin-on chicken thighs
1 bone-in, skin-on chicken drumstick
2 tablespoons Tandoori Paste (page 230)
¼ teaspoon sea salt
1 teaspoon fresh lemon juice or lemon dressing
100ml water
2–3 white bread slices

To serve
Onion & Coriander Salad (page 201)
Lemon wedges

- Using a sharp knife, pierce each piece of chicken several times. This will allow the marinade to properly flavour the chicken thighs and drumstick. Put the chicken pieces in a bowl, add the tandoori paste, sea salt and fresh lemon juice or lemon dressing, then mix well until the chicken is evenly coated. Cover and set aside in the refrigerator for 2 hours.

- Preheat the oven to 200°C/Gas 6 and line a baking tray with foil. Pour the water into the lined tray and press the bread slices down into the tray. This may seem odd but the bread and water will combine to soak up any drippings from the chicken as it cooks and your kitchen – and smoke alarm – will be grateful for this step!

- Place a wire rack over the lined baking tray, brush it lightly with a little vegetable oil and arrange the marinated chicken pieces on the rack. Bake the chicken for about 35 minutes, turning them once during cooking, until cooked through.

- Arrange the cooked chicken pieces on a serving plate and serve with onion and coriander salad and lemon wedges.

TANDOORI CHICKEN KEBAB
(INDIAN RESTAURANT STYLE)

This recipe can also be made with 2 boneless, skinless chicken thigh fillets – simply follow the method as described below, allowing an extra 1–2 minutes' cooking time.

Serves 1

    1 large boneless, skinless chicken breast fillet (about 150g)
    1½ tablespoons Tandoori Paste (page 230)
    Pinch of sea salt
    1 teaspoon fresh lemon juice or lemon dressing
    1 teaspoon vegetable oil

To serve
1 small handful fresh coriander leaves, finely chopped
Red Chilli Sauce (page 211)
1 Plain Chapati (page 170)

- Cut the chicken breast into 7–8 bite-sized pieces, put the pieces in a bowl, and add the tandoori paste, sea salt and fresh lemon juice or lemon dressing. Mix well, cover and set aside in the refrigerator for 2 hours.

- Heat a griddle pan or frying pan over a high heat. Lightly grease the pan with the vegetable oil. Carefully place the marinated chicken pieces in the pan, reduce the heat to medium-low and cook for 5–6 minutes, turning the chicken pieces occasionally until they are all cooked and just a little charred.

- Arrange the cooked tandoori chicken pieces on a serving plate, garnish with fresh coriander leaves and serve with red chilli sauce and a plain chapati.

TANDOORI KING PRAWNS (INDIAN RESTAURANT STYLE)

Serves 1–2

½ teaspoon cumin powder
½ teaspoon garam masala
½ teaspoon Kashmiri red chilli powder
Pinch of turmeric
1 teaspoon dried fenugreek leaves (methi)
½ teaspoon sea salt
120ml natural yogurt
1 tablespoon vegetable oil
1 teaspoon fresh lemon juice or lemon dressing
1 teaspoon Garlic Ginger Paste (page 228)
165g raw king prawns

To serve
Onion & Coriander Salad (page 201)
Garlic Sauce (page 213)

- Put the cumin powder, garam masala, red chilli powder, turmeric, dried fenugreek leaves, sea salt, natural yogurt, vegetable oil, fresh lemon juice or lemon dressing and garlic ginger paste in a bowl. Mix well. Add the king prawns and mix once more. Set aside for 15 minutes.

- Preheat the oven to 240°C/Gas 9. Wipe off any excess marinade from the prawns and arrange them on a baking tray. Bake the king prawns for 7–8 minutes or until the prawns are cooked through and sizzling.

- Arrange the cooked tandoori king prawns on a serving plate and serve with onion and coriander salad and garlic sauce.

PRAWNS FRY (TRADITIONAL INDIAN STYLE)

These prawns pack a spicy kick, and are perfect to serve alongside milder curry dishes such as Butter Curry (page 111) or Korma (page 103).

Serves 2

1 teaspoon Garlic Ginger Paste (page 228)
1 teaspoon vegetable oil
3 teaspoons fresh lemon juice or lemon dressing
½ teaspoon coriander powder
½ teaspoon garam masala
¾ teaspoon Kashmiri red chilli powder
¼ teaspoon turmeric
Generous pinch of sea salt
Generous pinch of ground black pepper
165g raw king prawns
1 tablespoon ghee (or vegetable oil)
½ teaspoon cumin seeds
1 small onion, finely chopped
1 fresh green finger chilli, thinly sliced
1½ tablespoons desiccated coconut
1 small handful fresh coriander leaves, finely chopped, to
   serve

- Put the garlic ginger paste, vegetable oil, 1 teaspoon of the fresh lemon juice or lemon dressing, coriander powder, garam masala, red chilli powder, turmeric, sea salt and black pepper in a bowl. Mix well. Add the king prawns and mix gently until all of the prawns are evenly coated in the marinade. Cover and set aside in the refrigerator for 1 hour.

- Heat the ghee in a curry pan or frying pan over a medium heat. Add the cumin seeds and chopped onion and stir-fry for 2 minutes until the onion begins to soften, then add the sliced green chilli and the marinated king prawns, discarding any excess marinade. Stir-fry for 3–4 minutes, or until the prawns change colour and are just cooked through. Add the desiccated coconut and stir-fry for a further 30 seconds. Add the remaining 2 teaspoons of fresh lemon juice or lemon dressing and mix a final time.

- Tip the prawns fry into a foil tray or onto a serving plate and garnish with the chopped coriander. Serve with your favourite curry dishes.

SEEKH KEBAB (INDIAN RESTAURANT STYLE)

Although the name of these kebabs refers to skewered meat, this recipe also works extremely well using the smashed burger method described below. Alternatively, if you have access to an outdoor grill, shape the mixture evenly across 6 flat kebab skewers and grill for 7–8 minutes, turning the skewers occasionally until the meat is just cooked through and charred nicely on the outside.

Serves 2–4 (Makes 4 seekh kebab patties)

450g lamb mince
1 medium onion, very finely chopped
1 fresh green finger chilli, finely chopped
2 teaspoons Garlic Ginger Paste (page 228)
1½ teaspoons cumin powder
1½ teaspoons coriander powder
1 teaspoon Kashmiri red chilli powder
Pinch of smoked paprika
1 teaspoon garam masala
1 small handful fresh coriander (stem and leaves), finely
    chopped
1 small handful fresh mint, finely chopped
1 teaspoon sea salt
¼ teaspoon ground black pepper

To serve
1 small handful fresh coriander leaves, finely chopped
Mint Sauce (page 214) or Raita (page 208)

- Put the lamb mince, chopped onion, fresh green chilli, garlic ginger paste, cumin powder, coriander powder, red chilli powder, smoked paprika, garam masala, fresh coriander, fresh mint, sea salt and black pepper in a large bowl. Mix thoroughly, punching your fist into the meat mixture and mixing well for 5 minutes until the ingredients are evenly mixed throughout the meat. Cover and set aside in the refrigerator for 2 hours or overnight.

- Divide the mixture into 4 equal pieces and shape into 4 large meatballs. Heat a dry frying pan over a medium-high heat. Place the seekh kebab meatball onto the pan and use a spatula wrapped in lightly oiled greaseproof paper to smash the meatball down into a large, thin burger-shaped patty. Reduce the heat to medium and cook the seekh kebab patty for about 3 minutes.

- Scrape underneath the patty with a flat spatula, carefully flip the patty and cook for a further 2 minutes. Set aside on a plate in the oven on a low heat to keep warm as you repeat the process and cook the remaining kebab patties.

- Arrange the cooked kebab patties on a serving plate, garnish with the fresh coriander and serve with mint sauce or raita.

LAMB CHOPS (INDIAN RESTAURANT STYLE)

If the weather is fair and the equipment available, cook or finish the lamb chops on a charcoal grill for a delicious smoky flavour.

Serves 1–2

1 teaspoon Garlic Ginger Paste (page 228)
1 fresh green finger chilli, thinly sliced
1 teaspoon garam masala
¼ teaspoon smoked paprika
Pinch of cumin powder
½ teaspoon sea salt
1 small handful fresh coriander leaves, finely chopped
50ml double cream
4 lamb chops, trimmed of excess fat
2 teaspoons vegetable oil, plus extra for basting

To serve
Carrot & Cashew Salad (page 202)
Mint Sauce (page 214)

- Put the garlic ginger paste, fresh green chilli, garam masala, smoked paprika, cumin powder, sea salt, fresh coriander leaves and double cream in a large bowl. Mix well.

- Add the lamb chops to the marinade and mix to coat. Cover and set aside in the refrigerator for at least 2 hours or, ideally, overnight.

- Remove the lamb chops from the refrigerator 20 minutes before cooking. Preheat the oven to 200°C/Gas 6. Add the oil to the lamb chops and mix well once more. Allow any excess marinade to drain off and arrange the lamb chops on a baking tray.

- Bake the lamb chops for 15 minutes. Turn, baste with a little extra vegetable oil and bake for a further 10–15 minutes until the lamb is cooked through and just beginning to char.

- Serve the lamb chops with carrot and cashew salad and mint sauce.

PUNJABI PURI (INDIAN RESTAURANT STYLE)

Cooked in a medium-spiced tasty curry sauce, this dish is essentially a half portion of curry, perfect for using up leftover cooked meat and vegetables.

Serves 1

150ml Curry Broth (pages 68 or 72)
½ teaspoon Garlic Ginger Paste (page 228)
½ teaspoon tomato purée
¼ teaspoon mild chilli powder
Pinch of beetroot powder (optional, for colour)
½ teaspoon dried fenugreek leaves (methi)
Pinch of sea salt
1 small handful fresh coriander leaves, finely chopped,
   plus extra to serve
Cooked meat/vegetables as desired

To serve
1 Puri Bread (page 174)
Onion & Coriander Salad (page 201)

- Put 4 tablespoons of the curry broth in a curry pan or frying pan and heat over a medium heat for 2–3 minutes until the sauce begins to sizzle.

- Add the garlic ginger paste, tomato purée, chilli powder, beetroot powder (if desired), dried fenugreek leaves, sea salt and fresh coriander. Add the cooked meat/vegetables as desired and about half of the remaining curry broth. Mix well and simmer for 2–3 minutes.

- Add the remaining curry broth and mix thoroughly. Cook for a further 2–3 minutes until the sauce reaches the desired consistency.

- Pour the Punjabi puri into a foil tray or onto a serving plate, garnish with fresh coriander and serve with puri bread and onion and coriander salad.

BOMBAY PURI

Cooked in a sweet and sour sauce, this tangy dish is essentially a half portion of patia curry sauce.

Serves 1

150ml Curry Broth (pages 68 or 72)
½ teaspoon Garlic Ginger Paste (page 228)
½ teaspoon tomato purée
¼ teaspoon mild chilli powder
Pinch of beetroot powder (optional, for colour)
½ teaspoon dried fenugreek leaves (methi)
Pinch of sea salt
1 small handful fresh coriander leaves, finely chopped
Cooked meat/vegetables as desired
1 tablespoon tomato ketchup
2 teaspoons mango chutney
1 teaspoon fresh lemon juice or lemon dressing

To serve
1 Puri Bread (page 174)
Onion & Coriander Salad (page 201)

- Put 4 tablespoons of the curry broth in a curry pan or frying pan and heat over a medium heat for 2–3 minutes until the sauce begins to sizzle.

- Add the garlic ginger paste, tomato purée, chilli powder, beetroot powder (if desired), dried fenugreek leaves, sea salt and fresh coriander. Add the cooked meat/vegetables as desired and about half of the remaining curry broth. Mix well and simmer for 2–3 minutes.

- Add the remaining curry broth and mix thoroughly. Cook for a further 2–3 minutes until the sauce reaches the desired consistency. Add the tomato ketchup, mango chutney and fresh lemon juice or lemon dressing and mix well once more. Simmer for 30 seconds.

- Pour the Bombay puri into a foil tray or onto a serving plate and serve with puri bread and onion and coriander salad.

RESTAURANT-STYLE CURRY DISHES

Indian restaurant curry dishes in the UK are far removed from authentic and traditional Indian cooking, and within the UK itself the dishes vary greatly from region to region based on customer tastes, the chef's background, experience and much more. Scotland's large Pakistani community has positively influenced many curry house dishes massively over the years.

In the kitchen of almost every Indian restaurant or takeaway in the UK you'll find a 'base gravy', 'gharabi' or 'curry base'. This huge bubbling pot made up of onions, onions and more onions, as well as spices and cooking oil, makes the restaurant chef's life far easier, the heavy lifting having already been done in the form of a vigorous cooking of the onions (adding natural sweetness), followed by a long, slow simmer, allowing the oil to fully cook out the spices. This sauce is then used to make different menu items, the skilled chef adding a few select ingredients depending on the flavour and heat level required.

Today, with a whole host of enthusiastic home cooks attempting to recreate their favourite curries at home, you'll find a wide variety of basic curry sauce recipes on forums online and in several books and YouTube videos. All of them will include the most important component – a mountain of onions – as well as a variety of other added ingredients and spices. You'll find curry base sauces with red and green peppers, carrots, fresh tomatoes, tinned tomatoes or no tomatoes at all. (Personally I prefer to include both fresh tomatoes and tomato passata.)

If you're eager to replicate a dish you've enjoyed in your local area, you're sure to find a friend or two online with equal ambitions and, with some shared knowledge and a little trial and error, you can customise recipes to more closely match the dishes you're looking for.

England-based Indian restaurants tend to favour a thinner curry sauce which is thickened with added spices (often referred to as 'mix powder') during the final cooking of the curry dish. Scottish Indian restaurants lean towards more of a concentrated, thick and toffee-like curry broth, which often requires thinning down with a little added water as the curry dishes themselves are cooked. The curry broth described in this book is very much in the Scottish Indian restaurant mould. It is a rich blend of onions, garlic, ginger, tomatoes and spices.

Following advice from Ohms (of the much-loved Dunfermline restaurant The Viceroy), I've settled on including tomatoes in three forms and have taken to utilising whole spices at the beginning of the process to infuse the cooking oil with aromatic flavours including green cardamom, cloves and cinnamon. The resultant broth is deliciously sweet and flavourful, just waiting to be turned into all manner of famous curry house sauces. Patia, Dansak, Nawabi . . . the list goes on and on!

CURRY BROTH — LARGE (INDIAN RESTAURANT STYLE)

This curry broth is well worth the effort to make and is the basis for many of the curry recipes in this book. Frozen in 250–300ml portions, it allows you to create your favourite curry dishes in a matter of minutes.

Makes about 3 litres (enough for 10–12 curry dishes)

Flavoured oil
300ml vegetable oil
2 Indian bay leaves
6 green cardamom pods, crushed
8 whole black peppercorns
6 cloves
¼ cinnamon stick or cassia bark

Broth
4kg onions, quartered (3kg peeled weight, about 20 of the largest onions you can find)
2 fresh salad tomatoes, quartered
2 garlic cloves, peeled but left whole
5cm piece of ginger (about the same size as the garlic)
1 teaspoon coriander seeds
1 teaspoon cumin seeds
2 litres water
100ml tomato passata

1½ tablespoons tomato purée
25g creamed coconut block
1 teaspoon garam masala
1½ tablespoons turmeric
½ teaspoon smoked paprika
½ teaspoon Kashmiri red chilli powder
1 generous tablespoon sea salt

- Pour the oil into a pan. Add the bay leaves, crushed green cardamom pods, black peppercorns, cloves and cinnamon stick or cassia bark. Heat the oil over a medium heat until the whole spices begin to bubble in the oil. Reduce the heat to low and allow the spices to infuse the oil for 5–6 minutes. Strain and set the oil aside.

- Put the quartered onions in a large stock pot and add the salad tomatoes, garlic cloves, ginger, coriander seeds, cumin seeds and water. Cover with a lid, bring to the boil and cook over a medium to high heat for 1 hour 20 minutes, stirring occasionally.

- Add the tomato passata, tomato purée, creamed coconut block, garam masala, turmeric, smoked paprika, red chilli powder and sea salt to the pot, stir well until the creamed coconut block is fully melted, then add the prepared flavoured oil. Mix well, cover and cook over a medium heat for a further 1 hour, stirring occasionally.

- Use a stick blender to blend the curry broth until completely smooth. Reduce the heat to the lowest setting and allow the curry broth to simmer for a further 1 hour, stirring occasionally until the broth becomes thick and toffee-like and the oil begins to separate. This long, slow simmering of the thick broth creates a delicious 'aged' flavour which will come through beautifully in your final curry dishes. Keep the broth almost fully covered with a lid during this stage of cooking and be cautious: as the curry thickens it will begin to spit and splutter.

- Allow the curry broth to cool completely then portion into 250–300ml containers or food bags. The curry can be refrigerated for up to 3 days and frozen for up to 3 months. I like to store the curry broth in the refrigerator for at least 24 hours before freezing, allowing the broth to mature a little before being stored. When you're ready to cook your curry, simply heat a portion of frozen curry base in a small pan over a medium heat for about 10 minutes until fully defrosted and use as per the recipe instructions.

Add your choice of the following to curry dishes:

Pre-cooked Chicken (pages 75 or 77)

Chicken Tikka (page 81)

Pre-cooked Lamb (page 79)

Lamb Tikka (page 81)

Paneer Cheese (page 233)

Mixed Vegetables – Frozen mixed vegetable 'steam' bags (carrot, broccoli, cauliflower, peas etc.) sold in supermarkets are ideal for quick vegetable curry dishes. Simply heat according to packet instructions and add to your favourite curry sauces.

Chickpeas – Tinned chickpeas are so convenient: simply rinse and drain before adding to simmering curry sauces.

CURRY BROTH – SMALL
(INDIAN RESTAURANT STYLE)

This smaller batch of curry broth is perfect if you don't have the freezer space to commit to making the full broth on the previous pages. This recipe makes enough for just 4 curry dishes, ideal for those weekend curry cravings.

Makes about 1 litre (enough for 4 curry dishes)

Flavoured oil
   100ml vegetable oil
   1 Indian bay leaf
   3 green cardamom pods, crushed
   4 whole black peppercorns
   3 cloves
   ⅛ cinnamon stick or cassia bark

Broth
   1kg onions, quartered (peeled weight, about 6–7 of the
      largest onions you can find)
   1 fresh salad tomato, quartered
   1 garlic clove
   2.5cm piece of ginger (about the same size as the garlic)
   ½ teaspoon coriander seeds
   ½ teaspoon cumin seeds
   1 litre water
   1½ teaspoons tomato purée

10g creamed coconut block
½ teaspoon garam masala
2 teaspoons turmeric
¼ teaspoon smoked paprika
¼ teaspoon Kashmiri red chilli powder
1 heaped teaspoon sea salt

- Pour the oil into a pan. Add the bay leaf, crushed green cardamom pods, black peppercorns, cloves and cinnamon stick or cassia bark. Heat the oil over a medium heat until the whole spices begin to bubble in the oil. Reduce the heat to low and allow the spices to infuse the oil for 5–6 minutes. Strain and set the oil aside.

- Put the quartered onions in a large stock pot and add the salad tomato, garlic clove, ginger, coriander seeds, cumin seeds and water. Cover with a lid, bring to the boil and cook over a medium to high heat for 45 minutes, stirring occasionally.

- Add the tomato purée, creamed coconut block, garam masala, turmeric, smoked paprika, red chilli powder and sea salt to the pot, stir well until the creamed coconut block is fully melted, then add the prepared flavoured oil. Mix well, reduce the heat to medium, cover and cook for another 45 minutes, stirring occasionally.

- Use a stick blender to blend the curry broth until completely smooth. Reduce the heat to the lowest setting and allow the curry broth to simmer for a further 30 minutes, stirring occasionally until the broth becomes thick and toffee-like and the oil begins to separate. This long, slow simmering of the thick broth creates a delicious 'aged' flavour which will come through beautifully in your final curry dishes. Keep the broth almost fully covered with a lid during this stage of cooking and be cautious – as the curry thickens it will begin to spit and splutter.

- Allow the curry broth to cool completely then portion into 250–300ml containers or food bags. The curry can be refrigerated for up to 3 days and frozen for up to 3 months.

CHICKEN FOR CURRY DISHES
(INDIAN RESTAURANT STYLE)

This simple spiced oil/stock ensures your chicken is both tender and aromatic, with beautiful background flavours of cloves, cardamom and cinnamon.

Makes enough chicken for 3 curry dishes (the recipe can be doubled, etc. if desired)

½ teaspoon cumin seeds
½ teaspoon coriander seeds
¼ teaspoon black peppercorns
2 green cardamom pods, crushed
2 cloves
¼ cinnamon stick or cassia bark
1 Indian bay leaf
¼ teaspoon garam masala
¼ teaspoon smoked paprika
½ teaspoon turmeric
¼ teaspoon beetroot powder (optional, for colour)
Pinch of dried fenugreek leaves (methi)
½ teaspoon sea salt
50ml vegetable oil
200ml water
2 large skinless, boneless chicken breasts (about 150g each), diced

- Put the cumin seeds, coriander seeds, black peppercorns, crushed green cardamom pods, cloves, cinnamon stick or cassia bark, bay leaf, garam masala, smoked paprika, turmeric, beetroot powder (if desired), dried fenugreek leaves, sea salt, vegetable oil and water in a pan. Mix well. Bring to the boil, reduce the heat to medium and allow the spices to simmer in the oil and water for 5 minutes.

- Add the diced chicken to the pot. Reduce the heat to medium-low and simmer for 20 minutes or until the chicken pieces are cooked through. Remove the pan from the heat and set aside to cool (leave the chicken in the spiced stock as it cools).

- Strain the chicken and discard the stock. The cooked chicken pieces are now ready to add to your favourite curry dishes. Alternatively, put the cooked chicken pieces in a container, cover and set aside in the refrigerator for up to 2 days or freeze for up to 3 months.

OVEN-BAKED CURRY CHICKEN

This oven method of pre-cooking chicken for curries is ideal if you're cooking up a curry feast, allowing you to keep your hob free for sauces and rice etc. while the chicken takes care of itself in the oven.

This recipe can be upscaled, providing the ingredient ratios are kept consistent, making it ideal for feeding a crowd. In theory your oven can be full of trays of cooked chicken while you cook several curry sauces on the hob.

Makes enough for 3 curry dishes

    2 large skinless, boneless chicken breast fillets (about 150g
        each)
    1 teaspoon Garlic Ginger Paste (page 228)
    1 teaspoon tomato purée
    ¼ teaspoon turmeric
    ½ teaspoon sea salt
    1 teaspoon vegetable oil
    1 teaspoon fresh lemon juice or lemon dressing
    ¼ teaspoon beetroot powder (optional, for colour)

• Preheat the oven to 150°C/Gas 2. Cut each chicken breast into 6 bite-sized pieces. Put the chicken in a bowl and add the garlic ginger paste, tomato purée, turmeric, sea salt, vegetable oil, fresh lemon juice or lemon dressing and beetroot powder (if desired). Mix well then transfer the chicken to a baking tray and separate the pieces so there is a little space between them.

- Bake the chicken for 20–22 minutes or until cooked through. The chicken can immediately be added to your curry dishes. Alternatively, set it aside to cool completely and store in portions in an airtight container in the refrigerator for up to 2 days, or in the freezer for up to 3 months.

LAMB FOR CURRY DISHES (INDIAN RESTAURANT STYLE)

Makes enough lamb for 3 curry dishes (the recipe can be doubled if desired)

½ teaspoon cumin seeds
½ teaspoon coriander seeds
¼ teaspoon black peppercorns
2 green cardamom pods, crushed
2 cloves
¼ cinnamon stick or cassia bark
1 Indian bay leaf
¼ teaspoon garam masala
¼ teaspoon smoked paprika
½ teaspoon turmeric
¼ teaspoon beetroot powder (optional, for colour)
Pinch of dried fenugreek leaves (methi)
½ teaspoon sea salt
50ml vegetable oil
200ml water
400g diced leg of lamb

- Put the cumin seeds, coriander seeds, black peppercorns, crushed green cardamom pods, cloves, cinnamon stick or cassia bark, bay leaf, garam masala, smoked paprika, turmeric, beetroot powder (if desired), dried fenugreek leaves, sea salt, vegetable oil and water in a pan. Mix well.

79

Bring to the boil, reduce the heat to medium and allow the spices to simmer in the oil and water for 5 minutes.

- Add the diced lamb to the pan. Reduce the heat to medium-low and simmer for 45 minutes or until the lamb pieces are tender. Remove the pan from the heat and set aside to cool (leave the lamb in the spiced stock as it cools).

- Strain the lamb and discard the stock. The cooked lamb pieces are now ready to add to your favourite curry dishes. Alternatively, put the cooked lamb pieces in a container, cover and set aside in the refrigerator for up to 2 days or freeze for up to 3 months.

CHICKEN OR LAMB TIKKA (INDIAN RESTAURANT STYLE)

These spiced meat pieces are cut fairly large for cooking but can be cut into smaller pieces after cooking and added to curry dishes as desired.

Makes enough tikka for about 8 curry dishes

- 6 large skinless, boneless chicken breast fillets (about 900g total weight) or equivalent weight lamb leg steaks
- 1½ tablespoons Tandoori Paste (page 230) or shop-bought tandoori or tikka paste
- 4 tablespoons natural yogurt
- 2 tablespoons vegetable oil
- 2 tablespoons fresh lemon juice or lemon dressing
- 1 teaspoon mint sauce
- ½ teaspoon beetroot powder (optional, for colour)
- ¼ teaspoon mild Madras curry powder
- ½ teaspoon coriander powder
- ¼ teaspoon cumin powder
- ½ teaspoon garam masala
- ½ teaspoon turmeric
- ¼ teaspoon Kashmiri red chilli powder
- 1 teaspoon dried fenugreek leaves (methi)
- 1 teaspoon sea salt
- 6 tablespoons water

To serve (optional)
Plain Chapati (page 170)
Traditional Curry Sauce (page 83)

- Trim any excess fat from the meat and cut each chicken breast or lamb leg steak into 3–4 pieces.

- Combine all the remaining ingredients in a large bowl. Mix thoroughly and add the meat, stirring it through the marinade to coat. Cover and marinate in the refrigerator for at least 2 hours, or overnight if possible.

- Preheat the oven to 200°C/Gas 6.

- Line a roasting tray with foil for easy clean up. Arrange the tikka pieces on a wire rack over the roasting tray and bake on the highest oven shelf for 7 minutes. Turn the tikka pieces and bake for a further 7 minutes. Turn the tikka pieces once more and bake for a further 5–6 minutes or until cooked through and just beginning to char.

- Serve the chicken or lamb tikka pieces with plain chapati and traditional curry sauce or use in your favourite curry sauces.

TRADITIONAL CURRY SAUCE
(INDIAN RESTAURANT STYLE)

This is a simple curry sauce, the sort you might expect to see served alongside tikka or tandoori dishes from restaurants and takeaways. The curry broth is infused with only a few basic curry ingredients, to create a mild flavour.

Serves 1–2

250–300ml Curry Broth (page 68 or page 72)
1 teaspoon Garlic Ginger Paste (page 228)
1 teaspoon tomato purée
¼ teaspoon Kashmiri red chilli powder
1 teaspoon dried fenugreek leaves (methi)
Pinch of sea salt
1 small handful fresh coriander leaves, finely chopped
Cooked meat/vegetables as desired

To serve
Small pinch of fresh coriander leaves, finely chopped
Cooked rice
Bread of choice
Poppadoms

- Heat 4 tablespoons of the curry broth in a curry pan or frying pan over a low to medium heat. Once the curry broth begins to sizzle, add the garlic ginger paste, tomato purée, red chilli powder, dried fenugreek leaves, sea salt and chopped fresh coriander leaves. Mix well and simmer for 1–2 minutes.

- Add the cooked meat/vegetables and about half of the remaining curry broth, mix well and allow to simmer for 2–3 minutes. As the sauce cooks you'll see it change in colour and the sauce will begin to caramelise. Add a little water if the curry broth becomes too thick too quickly.

- Add the remaining curry broth, mix once more and simmer for another 2–3 minutes until the sauce is slightly thick and bubbling hot. Pour the traditional curry sauce into a long foil tray or serving dish, garnish with a little more fresh coriander and serve with your favourite rice, bread and poppadoms.

MADRAS (INDIAN RESTAURANT STYLE)

A hot curry sauce containing lemon juice and, along with hot chilli powder, served with green chilli and a lemon slice on top.

Serves 1–2

2 fresh green finger chillies, thinly sliced (seeds and pith removed, or keep them in if you like it hot!)
Pinch of salt
2 teaspoons vegetable oil
250–300ml Curry Broth (page 68 or page 72)
1 teaspoon Garlic Ginger Paste (page 228)
1 teaspoon tomato purée
¼ teaspoon hot red chilli powder
1 teaspoon dried fenugreek leaves (methi)
1 small handful fresh coriander leaves, finely chopped
Cooked meat/vegetables as desired
1 teaspoon fresh lemon juice or lemon dressing

To serve
1 fresh lemon slice
Small pinch of fresh coriander leaves, finely chopped
Cooked rice
Bread of choice
Poppadoms

- Put the fresh green finger chillies in a pestle and mortar with the pinch of salt and carefully pound and mash the chillies to a paste (be careful and look the other way to avoid any chilli splashback!). Add the vegetable oil, mix and set aside.

- Heat 4 tablespoons of the curry broth in a curry pan or frying pan over a low to medium heat. Once the curry broth begins to sizzle, add the garlic ginger paste, tomato purée, hot red chilli powder, dried fenugreek leaves and chopped fresh coriander leaves. Mix well and simmer for 1–2 minutes.

- Add the cooked meat/vegetables as desired, the prepared green chilli paste and about half of the remaining curry broth, mix well and allow to simmer for 2–3 minutes. As the sauce cooks you'll see it change in colour and the sauce will begin to caramelise. Add just a little water if the curry broth becomes too thick too quickly.

- Add the remaining curry broth, mix once more and simmer for another 2–3 minutes until the sauce is slightly thick and bubbling hot. Add the fresh lemon juice or lemon dressing and mix once more. Pour the madras curry sauce into a long foil tray or serving dish, top with the lemon slice, garnish with fresh coriander and serve with your favourite rice, bread and poppadoms.

VINDALOO (INDIAN RESTAURANT STYLE)

The king of the hot curries, served with fresh coriander, spring onion and a lemon slice on top.

Serves 1–2

3 fresh green finger chillies, thinly sliced (seeds and pith removed, or keep them in if you like it hot!)
Pinch of sea salt
2 teaspoons vegetable oil
250–300ml Curry Broth (page 68 or page 72)
1 teaspoon Garlic Ginger Paste (page 228)
1 teaspoon tomato purée
½ teaspoon extra hot red chilli powder
Pinch of beetroot powder (optional, for colour)
1 teaspoon dried fenugreek leaves (methi)
1 small handful fresh coriander leaves, finely chopped
Cooked meat/vegetables as desired

To serve
1 fresh lemon slice
Small pinch of fresh coriander leaves, finely chopped
½ spring onion, thinly sliced
Cooked rice
Bread of choice
Poppadoms

- Put the fresh green finger chillies in a pestle and mortar with the pinch of salt and carefully pound and mash the chillies to a paste (be careful and look the other way to avoid any chilli splashback!). Add the vegetable oil, mix and set aside.

- Heat 4 tablespoons of the curry broth in a curry pan or frying pan over a low to medium heat. Once the curry broth begins to sizzle, add the garlic ginger paste, tomato purée, extra hot red chilli powder, beetroot powder (if desired), dried fenugreek leaves and chopped fresh coriander leaves. Mix well and simmer for 1–2 minutes.

- Add the cooked meat/vegetables as desired, the prepared green chilli paste and about half of the remaining curry broth, mix well and allow to simmer for 2–3 minutes. As the sauce cooks you'll see it change in colour and the sauce will begin to caramelise. Add just a little water if the curry broth becomes too thick too quickly.

- Add the remaining curry broth, mix once more and simmer for another 2–3 minutes until the sauce is slightly thick and bubbling hot. Pour the vindaloo curry sauce into a long foil tray or serving dish, top with the lemon slice, garnish with a little more fresh coriander and thinly sliced spring onion and serve with your favourite rice, bread and poppadoms.

JALFREZI (INDIAN RESTAURANT STYLE)

A mild, creamy dish made with peppers, onions, coconut cream and ground cashews.

Serves 1–2

2 teaspoons vegetable oil
1 onion, sliced
¼ red pepper, cut into 1cm-thick slices
¼ green pepper, cut into 1cm-thick slices
1 salad tomato, quartered
¼ teaspoon cumin seeds
1 fresh green finger chilli, sliced (optional)
250–300ml Curry Broth (page 68 or page 72)
1 teaspoon Garlic Ginger Paste (page 228)
½ teaspoon tomato purée
¼ teaspoon Kashmiri red chilli powder
Pinch of beetroot powder (optional, for colour)
Pinch of sea salt
Small handful fresh coriander leaves, finely chopped
Cooked meat/vegetables as desired
2 teaspoons cashew butter
15g creamed coconut block

To serve
½ teaspoon flaked almonds
Small pinch of fresh coriander leaves, finely chopped

Cooked rice
Bread of choice
Poppadoms

- Heat the oil in a curry pan or frying pan over a medium heat. Add the sliced onion, red pepper, green pepper and tomato and stir-fry for 2 minutes. Add the cumin seeds and sliced green chilli (if desired) and stir-fry for a further 30 seconds, then add 4 tablespoons of the curry broth and mix well. Add the garlic ginger paste, tomato purée, red chilli powder, beetroot powder (if desired), sea salt and fresh coriander. Mix well and allow the sauce to simmer for 2–3 minutes.

- Add the cooked meat/vegetables as desired and about half of the remaining curry broth. Mix well and simmer for 2–3 minutes. As the sauce cooks you'll see it change in colour and the sauce will begin to caramelise. Add just a little water if the curry broth becomes too thick too quickly.

- Add the remaining curry broth, the cashew butter and creamed coconut, stirring well until the creamed coconut block is fully melted. Mix well and simmer for another 2–3 minutes until the sauce is slightly thick and bubbling hot. Pour the jalfrezi curry sauce into a long foil tray or serving dish, top with the flaked almonds, garnish with fresh coriander and serve with your favourite rice, bread and poppadoms.

BHUNA (INDIAN RESTAURANT STYLE)

A medium-spiced dry dish with tomatoes.

Serves 1–2

   1 teaspoon vegetable oil
   ¼ teaspoon cumin seeds
   1 small onion, finely chopped
   1 salad tomato, quartered
   200ml Curry Broth (page 68 or page 72)
   1 teaspoon Garlic Ginger Paste (page 228)
   1 fresh green finger chilli, thinly sliced, seeds and pith
      removed (or keep them in if you like it hot!)
   1 teaspoon tomato purée
   ¼ teaspoon Kashmiri red chilli powder
   1 teaspoon dried fenugreek leaves (methi)
   Pinch of sea salt
   1 small handful fresh coriander leaves, finely chopped
   Cooked meat/vegetables as desired

To serve
Small pinch of fresh coriander leaves, finely chopped
Cooked rice
Bread of choice
Poppadoms

- Heat the oil in a curry pan or frying pan over a medium heat. Add the cumin seeds, chopped onion and salad tomato and stir-fry for 1 minute. Add 4 tablespoons of the curry broth. Once the curry broth begins to sizzle, add the garlic ginger paste, fresh green chilli, tomato purée, red chilli powder, dried fenugreek leaves, sea salt and chopped fresh coriander leaves. Mix well and simmer for 1–2 minutes.

- Add the cooked meat/vegetables as desired and about half of the remaining curry broth, mix well and allow to simmer for 2–3 minutes. As the sauce cooks you'll see it change in colour and the sauce will begin to caramelise.

- Add the remaining curry broth, mix once more and simmer for another 2–3 minutes until the sauce is thick and bubbling hot. Pour the bhuna curry sauce into a long foil tray or serving dish, garnish with a little more fresh coriander and serve with your favourite rice, bread and poppadoms.

DOPIAZA (INDIAN RESTAURANT STYLE)

An aromatic dish with extra fried onions.

Serves 1–2

2 teaspoons vegetable oil
1 small onion, roughly chopped
250–300ml Curry Broth (page 68 or page 72)
1 teaspoon Garlic Ginger Paste (page 228)
1 teaspoon tomato purée
¼ teaspoon Kashmiri red chilli powder
1 teaspoon dried fenugreek leaves (methi)
Pinch of sea salt
1 small handful fresh coriander leaves, finely chopped
Cooked meat/vegetables as desired

To serve
½ small onion, very thinly sliced
Cooked rice
Bread of choice
Poppadoms

- Heat the oil in a curry pan or large frying pan over a medium heat, add the chopped onion and stir-fry for 2 minutes. Add 4 tablespoons of the curry broth and mix well. Add the garlic ginger paste, tomato purée, red chilli powder, dried fenugreek leaves, sea salt and chopped fresh coriander leaves. Mix well and simmer for 1–2 minutes.

- Add the cooked meat/vegetables as desired and about half of the remaining curry broth, mix well and allow to simmer for 2–3 minutes. As the sauce cooks you'll see it change in colour and the sauce will begin to caramelise. Add 1–2 tablespoons of water if the curry broth becomes too thick too quickly.

- Add the remaining curry broth, mix once more and simmer for another 2–3 minutes until the sauce is slightly thick and bubbling hot. Pour the dopiaza curry sauce into a long foil tray or serving dish, garnish with thinly sliced onion and serve with your favourite rice, bread and poppadoms.

JAIPURI (INDIAN RESTAURANT STYLE)

A medium-hot tasty fusion of chunky green peppers, mushrooms and onion.

Serves 1–2

2 teaspoons vegetable oil
½ small onion, sliced
¼ green pepper, sliced
2–3 small button mushrooms, cut into 5mm-thick
   slices
250–300ml Curry Broth (page 68 or page 72)
1 teaspoon Garlic Ginger Paste (page 228)
1 teaspoon tomato purée
¼ teaspoon mild chilli powder
1 teaspoon dried fenugreek leaves (methi)
Pinch of sea salt
1 small handful fresh coriander leaves, finely chopped
Cooked meat/vegetables as desired
1 tablespoon single cream

To serve
Pinch of fresh coriander leaves, finely chopped
Cooked rice
Bread of choice
Poppadoms

- Heat the oil in a curry pan or large frying pan over a medium heat, add the sliced onion, green pepper and mushrooms and stir-fry for 2 minutes. Add 4 tablespoons of the curry broth and mix well. Add the garlic ginger paste, tomato purée, mild chilli powder, dried fenugreek leaves, sea salt and chopped fresh coriander leaves. Mix well and simmer for 1–2 minutes.

- Add the cooked meat/vegetables as desired and about half of the remaining curry broth, mix well and allow to simmer for 2–3 minutes. As the sauce cooks you'll see it change in colour and the sauce will begin to caramelise. Add 1–2 tablespoons of water if the curry broth becomes too thick too quickly.

- Add the remaining curry broth and single cream, mix once more and simmer for another 2–3 minutes until the sauce is slightly thick and bubbling hot. Pour the Jaipuri curry sauce into a long foil tray or serving dish, garnish with a little more fresh coriander and serve with your favourite rice, bread and poppadoms.

DANSAK (INDIAN RESTAURANT STYLE)

A slightly sweet dish with pineapple and red lentils.

Serves 1–2

50g red lentils, washed and drained
Pinch of turmeric
200ml water
250–300ml Curry Broth (page 68 or page 72)
1 teaspoon Garlic Ginger Paste (page 228)
1 teaspoon tomato purée
¼ teaspoon Kashmiri red chilli powder
1 teaspoon dried fenugreek leaves (methi)
Pinch of sea salt
1 small handful fresh coriander leaves, finely chopped
Cooked meat/vegetables as desired
2 tablespoons pineapple juice
40g pineapple, roughly chopped (1 average ring of pineapple from a tin)
1 teaspoon fresh lemon juice or lemon dressing

To serve
Small pinch of fresh coriander leaves, finely chopped
Cooked rice
Bread of choice
Poppadoms

- Put the lentils in a pan with the turmeric and water. Bring to the boil, reduce the heat to low and simmer for about 30 minutes, or until the lentils are soft. Set aside to cool for 20 minutes. Alternatively, cool completely and set aside covered in the refrigerator for up to 2 days, until required.

- Heat 4 tablespoons of the curry broth in a curry pan or frying pan over a low to medium heat. Once the curry broth begins to sizzle, add the garlic ginger paste, tomato purée, red chilli powder, dried fenugreek leaves, sea salt and chopped fresh coriander leaves. Mix well and simmer for 1–2 minutes.

- Add the cooked meat/vegetables as desired and about half of the remaining curry broth, mix well and allow to simmer for 2–3 minutes. As the sauce cooks you'll see it change in colour and the sauce will begin to caramelise. Add the cooked lentils, pineapple juice and chopped pineapple.

- Add the remaining curry broth, mix once more and simmer for another 2–3 minutes until the sauce is slightly thick and bubbling hot. Add the fresh lemon juice or lemon dressing and mix once more. Pour the dansak curry sauce into a long foil tray or serving dish, garnish with a little more fresh coriander and serve with your favourite rice, bread and poppadoms.

PATIA (INDIAN RESTAURANT STYLE)

A sauce cooked with mango, lemon juice and tomatoes for a sweet and sour taste.

Serves 1–2

250–300ml Curry Broth (page 68 or page 72)
1 teaspoon Garlic Ginger Paste (page 228)
1 teaspoon tomato purée
¼ teaspoon mild red chilli powder
1 teaspoon dried fenugreek leaves (methi)
Pinch of sea salt
1 small handful fresh coriander leaves, finely chopped
Cooked meat/vegetables as desired
2 tablespoons tomato ketchup
1 tablespoon mango chutney
2 teaspoons fresh lemon juice or lemon dressing
¼ teaspoon beetroot powder (optional, for colour)

To serve
Small pinch of fresh coriander leaves, finely chopped
Cooked rice
Bread of choice
Poppadoms

- Heat 4 tablespoons of the curry broth in a curry pan or frying pan over a low to medium heat. Once the curry broth begins to sizzle, add the garlic ginger paste, tomato purée, red chilli powder, dried fenugreek leaves, sea salt and chopped fresh coriander leaves. Mix well and simmer for 1–2 minutes.

- Add the cooked meat/vegetables as desired and about half of the remaining curry broth, mix well and allow to simmer for 2–3 minutes. As the sauce cooks you'll see it change in colour and the sauce will begin to caramelise.

- Add the remaining curry broth, mix once more and simmer for another 2–3 minutes until the sauce is slightly thick and bubbling hot. Add the tomato ketchup, mango chutney, fresh lemon juice or lemon dressing and beetroot powder (if desired). Mix well and simmer for a further 1 minute. Pour the patia sauce into a long foil tray or serving dish, garnish with a little more fresh coriander and serve with your favourite rice, bread and poppadoms.

CHASNI (INDIAN RESTAURANT STYLE)

A tangy sauce, creamy and sour with mild spices and lemon.

Serves 1–2

2 tablespoons tomato ketchup
1 tablespoon mango chutney
½ teaspoon mint sauce
2 teaspoons fresh lemon juice or lemon dressing
¼ teaspoon beetroot powder
250–300ml Curry Broth (page 68 or page 72)
1 teaspoon Garlic Ginger Paste (page 228)
1 teaspoon tomato purée
¼ teaspoon Kashmiri red chilli powder
1 teaspoon dried fenugreek leaves (methi)
Pinch of sea salt
1 small handful fresh coriander leaves, finely
    chopped
Cooked meat/vegetables as desired
1 teaspoon ground almonds
100ml single cream

To serve
Cooked rice
Bread of choice
Poppadoms

- Put the tomato ketchup, mango chutney, mint sauce, fresh lemon juice or lemon dressing and beetroot powder in a bowl. Mix well and set aside.

- Heat 4 tablespoons of the curry broth in a curry pan or frying pan over a low to medium heat. Once the curry broth begins to sizzle, add the garlic ginger paste, tomato purée, red chilli powder, dried fenugreek leaves, sea salt and chopped fresh coriander leaves. Mix well and simmer for 1–2 minutes.

- Add the cooked meat/vegetables as desired and about half of the remaining curry broth, mix well and allow to simmer for 2–3 minutes. As the sauce cooks you'll see it change in colour and the sauce will begin to caramelise. Add 1 tablespoon of water if the curry broth becomes too thick too quickly.

- Add the remaining curry broth and the prepared ketchup/mango chutney mix. Add the ground almonds and single cream, stir once more and simmer for another 2–3 minutes until the sauce is slightly thick and bubbling hot. Pour the chasni sauce into a long foil tray or serving dish and serve with your favourite rice, bread and poppadoms.

KORMA (INDIAN RESTAURANT STYLE)

A mild and slightly sweet dish, with cream and coconut.

Serves 1–2

2 teaspoons coconut flour
2 teaspoons caster sugar
2 teaspoons ground almonds
Pinch of sea salt
100ml water
250ml Curry Broth (page 68 or page 72)
Cooked meat/vegetables as desired
25g creamed coconut block
75ml single cream

To serve
1 teaspoon single cream
Poppadoms (page 215)

- Put the coconut flour, caster sugar, ground almonds, sea salt and water in a bowl. Mix well and set aside.

- Heat 4 tablespoons of the curry broth in a curry pan or frying pan over a medium heat. Once the sauce begins to sizzle, add about half of the remaining curry broth. Simmer for 2 minutes.

- Add the remaining curry broth and cooked meat/vegetables as desired and simmer the korma sauce for 2–3 minutes, stirring occasionally. Add the prepared coconut, sugar and almond mix and mix well. Simmer for 2–3 minutes.

- Add the creamed coconut block and single cream, stirring well until the creamed coconut block is fully melted. Mix well and simmer for a further 1–2 minutes. Pour the korma into a foil tray or serving dish, top with the teaspoon of single cream and serve with poppadoms.

Variations

Desi Korma – Add 1 teaspoon cashew butter, 50ml of coconut milk and 1 teaspoon of salted butter to the pan along with the creamed coconut block and single cream.

Kashmiri Korma – Add 7–8 pieces of sliced banana, pineapple or mango to the pan along with the creamed coconut block and single cream.

Parsee Korma – Add 1 teaspoon ground pistachios and finish with 1 teaspoon fresh lemon juice or lemon dressing to the pan along with the creamed coconut block and single cream.

Punjabi Korma – Add 1 teaspoon cashew butter, 1 tablespoon white wine and a small handful of fresh coriander leaves, finely chopped, to the pan along with the creamed coconut block and single cream.

TIKKA MASALA (INDIAN RESTAURANT STYLE)

Serves 1–2

250–300ml Curry Broth (page 68 or page 72)
1 teaspoon Garlic Ginger Paste (page 228)
1 teaspoon tomato purée
¼ teaspoon Kashmiri red chilli powder
1 teaspoon dried fenugreek leaves (methi)
Pinch of sea salt
1 small handful fresh coriander leaves, finely
    chopped
1 teaspoon Tandoori Paste (page 230) or shop-bought
    tandoori or tikka paste
1 teaspoon caster sugar
1 teaspoon ground almonds
½ teaspoon beetroot powder (optional, for colour)
Cooked meat/vegetables as desired
100ml single cream
1–2 tablespoons water
1 teaspoon fresh lemon juice or lemon dressing

To serve
Small pinch of fresh coriander leaves, finely chopped
Cooked rice
Bread of choice
Poppadoms

- Heat 4 tablespoons of curry broth in a curry pan or frying pan over a low to medium heat. Once the curry broth begins to sizzle, add the garlic ginger paste, tomato purée, red chilli powder, dried fenugreek leaves, sea salt and chopped fresh coriander leaves. Mix well and simmer for 1–2 minutes.

- Add the tandoori paste, sugar, ground almonds and beetroot powder (if desired), then add the cooked meat/vegetables as desired and about half of the remaining curry broth. Mix well and allow to simmer for 2–3 minutes. As the sauce cooks you'll see it change in colour and the sauce will begin to caramelise. Add a little water if the curry broth becomes too thick too quickly.

- Add the remaining curry broth, single cream and water, mix once more and simmer for another 2–3 minutes until the sauce is slightly thick and bubbling hot. Add the fresh lemon juice or lemon dressing and mix once more. Pour the tikka masala curry into a long foil tray or serving dish, garnish with a little more fresh coriander and serve with your favourite rice, bread and poppadoms.

CHEF'S SPECIALS

An Indian takeaway or restaurant menu typically offers 'old favourites' or 'classics' – dishes such as madras, korma and patia, which are based on quick and easy adaptations to the restaurant curry broth. Conversely, 'Chef's Special' dishes utilise a larger variety of added ingredients and require more time and attention by the chef, hence these dishes are usually more expensive and not included as part of restaurant 'meal deals'.

SOUTH INDIAN GARLIC CHILLI
(INDIAN RESTAURANT STYLE)

A garlic chilli sauce with fresh coriander, garnished with a topping of green chillies and spring onion.

Serves 1–2

- 3 fresh green finger chillies, thinly sliced (seeds and pith removed, or keep them in if you like it hot!)
- Pinch of sea salt
- 3 teaspoons vegetable oil
- 1 small onion, finely chopped
- ¼ red pepper, finely chopped
- ¼ green pepper, finely chopped
- 250ml Curry Broth (page 68 or page 72)
- 1 teaspoon Garlic Ginger Paste (page 228)
- 1 teaspoon tomato purée
- ¼ teaspoon Kashmiri red chilli powder
- ¼ teaspoon beetroot powder (optional, for colour)
- 1 teaspoon dried fenugreek leaves (methi)
- 1 small handful fresh coriander leaves, finely chopped
- Cooked meat/vegetables as desired
- 50ml single cream
- 1 teaspoon ground almonds
- 1 teaspoon cashew butter
- 1 teaspoon salted butter

¼ teaspoon garlic powder
Small pinch of garam masala

To serve
1 teaspoon single cream
Small pinch of fresh coriander leaves, finely chopped
1 green finger chilli, sliced lengthways
½ spring onion, thinly sliced
Cooked rice
Bread of choice
Poppadoms

- Put the fresh green finger chillies in a pestle and mortar with the pinch of salt. Carefully pound and mash the chillies to a paste (be careful and look the other way to avoid any chilli splashback!). Add 1 teaspoon of the vegetable oil, mix and set aside.

- Heat the remaining 2 teaspoons of vegetable oil in a curry pan or frying pan over a medium heat, add the chopped onion, red pepper and green pepper and stir-fry for 2–3 minutes until the vegetables begin to soften. Add 4 tablespoons of the curry broth and mix well. Add the garlic ginger paste, tomato purée, red chilli powder, beetroot powder (if desired), dried fenugreek leaves and chopped fresh coriander leaves. Mix well and simmer for 1–2 minutes.

- Add the cooked meat/vegetables as desired and about half of the remaining curry broth, mix well and allow to simmer for 2–3 minutes. As the sauce cooks you'll see it change in colour and the sauce will begin to caramelise.

- Add the remaining curry broth to the pan, along with the single cream, prepared green chilli mix, ground almonds, cashew butter, salted butter and garlic powder. Mix once more and simmer for another 2–3 minutes until the sauce is slightly thick and bubbling hot. Add the garam masala and mix through. Pour the curry into a long foil tray or serving dish, drizzle over the single cream, top with fresh coriander, sliced green chilli and spring onion and serve with your favourite rice, bread and poppadoms.

BUTTER CURRY (INDIAN RESTAURANT STYLE)

A mild dish with tomatoes and cream combining to create a rich and slightly sweet flavour.

Serves 1–2

250ml Curry Broth (page 68 or page 72)
1 teaspoon Garlic Ginger Paste (page 228)
1 teaspoon tomato purée
¼ teaspoon Kashmiri red chilli powder
1 teaspoon dried fenugreek leaves (methi)
Pinch of sea salt
1 small handful fresh coriander leaves, finely chopped
Cooked meat/vegetables as desired
100ml condensed cream of tomato soup
¼ teaspoon beetroot powder (optional, for colour)
1½ teaspoons ground almonds
½ teaspoon caster sugar
75ml water
1 tablespoon single cream
1 teaspoon ghee

To serve
1 teaspoon salted butter
Pinch of garam masala
Cooked rice
Bread of choice
Poppadoms

- Heat 4 tablespoons of the curry broth in a curry pan or frying pan over a low to medium heat. Once the curry broth begins to sizzle, add the garlic ginger paste, tomato purée, red chilli powder, dried fenugreek leaves, sea salt and chopped fresh coriander leaves. Mix well and simmer for 1–2 minutes.

- Add the cooked meat/vegetables as desired and about half of the remaining curry broth, mix well and allow to simmer for 2–3 minutes. As the sauce cooks you'll see it change in colour and the sauce will begin to caramelise.

- Add the remaining curry broth, condensed cream of tomato soup, beetroot powder (if desired), ground almonds, caster sugar, water, single cream and ghee, mix well and simmer for another 3–4 minutes until the sauce is slightly thick and bubbling hot. Pour the butter curry sauce into a long foil tray or serving dish, top with 1 teaspoon of salted butter and the pinch of garam masala and serve with your favourite rice, bread and poppadoms.

ACHARI (INDIAN RESTAURANT STYLE)

A sour and spicy special curry with fresh green pepper, onion and mixed pickle.

Serves 1–2

2 teaspoons vegetable oil

1 small onion, roughly chopped

½ green pepper, roughly chopped

250–300ml Curry Broth (page 68 or page 72)

1 teaspoon Garlic Ginger Paste (page 228)

1 fresh green finger chilli, thinly sliced (seeds and pith removed, or leave them in if you like it hot!)

1 teaspoon tomato purée

¼ teaspoon Kashmiri red chilli powder

1 teaspoon dried fenugreek leaves (methi)

Pinch of sea salt

1 small handful fresh coriander leaves, finely chopped

Cooked meat/vegetables as desired

1 teaspoon ground almonds

2 tablespoons tomato ketchup

1 teaspoon mango chutney

1 heaped teaspoon mixed pickle (I like the Ashoka brand)

50ml single cream

1 teaspoon fresh lemon juice or lemon dressing

To serve
Small pinch of fresh coriander leaves, finely chopped
Cooked rice
Bread of choice
Poppadoms

- Heat the oil in a curry pan or frying pan over a medium heat, add the chopped onion and green pepper and stir-fry for 2 minutes. Add 4 tablespoons of the curry broth and once the curry broth begins to sizzle, add the garlic ginger paste, green chilli, tomato purée, red chilli powder, dried fenugreek leaves, sea salt and chopped fresh coriander leaves. Mix well and simmer for 1–2 minutes.

- Add the cooked meat/vegetables as desired and about half of the remaining curry broth, mix well and allow to simmer for 2–3 minutes. As the sauce cooks you'll see it change in colour and the sauce will begin to caramelise. Add a little water if the curry broth becomes too thick too quickly.

- Add the remaining curry broth, ground almonds, tomato ketchup, mango chutney and mixed pickle, mix once more and simmer for another 1 minute. Add the single cream and fresh lemon juice or lemon dressing, mix once more and simmer for a further 2 minutes until the sauce is slightly thick and bubbling hot. Pour the achari curry sauce into a long foil tray or serving dish, garnish with a little more fresh coriander and serve with your favourite rice, bread and poppadoms.

NAWABI (INDIAN RESTAURANT STYLE)

A special dish from Moghul India, mild with cashew butter, almonds, fresh cream and dried fruits.

Serves 1–2

1 handful mixed nuts, roughly chopped (shelled pistachios, almonds, cashews, hazelnuts)
5 or 6 sultanas
2 dried apricots, roughly chopped
250–300ml Curry Broth (page 68 or page 72)
1 teaspoon Garlic Ginger Paste (page 228)
1 teaspoon tomato purée
¼ teaspoon Kashmiri red chilli powder
1 teaspoon dried fenugreek leaves (methi)
Pinch of sea salt
1 small handful fresh coriander leaves, finely chopped
Cooked meat/vegetables as desired
1 teaspoon cashew butter
1 teaspoon ground almonds
2 tablespoons single cream
1 teaspoon caster sugar
10g creamed coconut block

To serve
Small pinch of fresh coriander leaves, finely chopped
Cooked rice

Bread of choice
Poppadoms

- Mix the roughly chopped mixed nuts, sultanas and dried apricots in a bowl. Set aside.

- Heat 4 tablespoons of the curry broth in a curry pan or frying pan over a low to medium heat. Once the curry broth begins to sizzle, add the garlic ginger paste, tomato purée, red chilli powder, dried fenugreek leaves, sea salt and chopped fresh coriander leaves. Mix well and simmer for 1–2 minutes.

- Add the cooked meat/vegetables as desired and about half of the remaining curry broth. Mix well and allow to simmer for 2–3 minutes. As the sauce cooks you'll see it change in colour and the sauce will begin to caramelise. Add a splash of water if the curry broth becomes too thick too quickly.

- Add the remaining curry broth, cashew butter, ground almonds, single cream and sugar and about half of the fruit and nut mix. Mix well and simmer for another 2–3 minutes until the sauce is slightly thick and bubbling hot. Add the creamed coconut and stir well until the creamed coconut block is fully melted. Pour the nawabi sauce into a long foil tray or serving dish, garnish with fresh coriander and top with the remaining fruit and nut mix. Serve with your favourite rice, bread and poppadoms.

SHARABI (INDIAN RESTAURANT STYLE)

Cooked with a touch of Scotch whisky, this is a dish to welcome you home in the evening.

Serves 1–2

2 fresh green finger chillies, thinly sliced (seeds and pith removed, or keep them in if you like it hot!)
Pinch of sea salt
3 teaspoons vegetable oil
1 small onion, finely chopped
½ green pepper, finely chopped
1 salad tomato, deseeded and roughly chopped
250ml Curry Broth (page 68 or page 72)
1 teaspoon Garlic Ginger Paste (page 228)
1 teaspoon tomato purée
¼ teaspoon Kashmiri red chilli powder
¼ teaspoon beetroot powder (optional, for colour)
Pinch of cinnamon powder
1 teaspoon dried fenugreek leaves (methi)
1 small handful fresh coriander leaves, finely chopped
Cooked meat/vegetables as desired
1 tablespoon tomato ketchup
1 tablespoon Scotch whisky
Pinch of garam masala

To serve
Small pinch of fresh coriander leaves, finely chopped
Cooked rice
Bread of choice
Poppadoms

- Put the fresh green finger chillies in a pestle and mortar with the pinch of salt. Carefully pound and mash the chillies to a paste (be careful and look the other way to avoid any chilli splashback!). Add 1 teaspoon of the vegetable oil, mix and set aside.

- Heat the remaining 2 teaspoons of vegetable oil in a curry pan or frying pan over a medium heat. Add the chopped onion, green pepper and tomato and stir-fry for 2–3 minutes until the vegetables begin to soften. Add 4 tablespoons of the curry broth and mix well, then add the garlic ginger paste, tomato purée, red chilli powder, beetroot powder (if desired), cinnamon powder, dried fenugreek leaves and chopped fresh coriander leaves. Mix well and simmer for 1–2 minutes.

- Add the cooked meat/vegetables as desired and about half of the remaining curry broth. Mix well and allow to simmer for 2–3 minutes. As the sauce cooks you'll see it change in colour and the sauce will begin to caramelise. Add 1 tablespoon of water if the curry broth becomes too thick too quickly.

- Add the remaining curry broth and the prepared green chilli paste. Mix well and simmer for another 2–3 minutes until the sauce is slightly thick and bubbling hot. Add the tomato ketchup and mix well. Add the Scotch whisky and garam masala, mix once more and simmer for a further 1 minute. Pour the sharabi curry into a long foil tray or serving dish, garnish with fresh coriander and serve with your favourite rice, bread and poppadoms.

CEYLONESE (INDIAN RESTAURANT STYLE)

Serves 1–2

2 fresh green finger chillies, thinly sliced (seeds and pith removed, or keep them in if you like it hot!)

Pinch of sea salt

3 teaspoons vegetable oil

1 dried red chilli, cut into 2 pieces

¼ teaspoon extra hot crushed chillies

250–300ml Curry Broth (page 68 or page 72)

1 teaspoon Garlic Ginger Paste (page 228)

1 teaspoon tomato purée

¼ teaspoon Kashmiri red chilli powder

1 teaspoon dried fenugreek leaves (methi)

1 small handful fresh coriander leaves, finely chopped

Cooked meat/vegetables as desired

1 teaspoon mango chutney

1 teaspoon ground almonds

1 teaspoon cashew butter

1 teaspoon coconut flour

1 teaspoon caster sugar

25g creamed coconut block

100ml water

2 teaspoons fresh lemon juice or lemon dressing

To serve

Small pinch of fresh coriander leaves, finely chopped

Cooked rice

Bread of choice
Poppadoms

- Put the fresh green finger chillies in a pestle and mortar with the pinch of salt. Carefully pound and mash the chillies to a paste (be careful and look the other way to avoid any chilli splashback!). Add 1 teaspoon of the vegetable oil, mix and set aside.

- Heat the remaining 2 teaspoons of vegetable oil in a curry pan or frying pan over a medium heat. Add the dried red chilli pieces and crushed chillies. Stir-fry for 20–30 seconds until the red chilli begins to darken, then add 4 tablespoons of curry broth. Once the curry broth begins to sizzle, add the garlic ginger paste, tomato purée, red chilli powder, dried fenugreek leaves and chopped fresh coriander leaves. Mix well and simmer for 1–2 minutes.

- Add the cooked meat/vegetables as desired and about half of the remaining curry broth, mix well and allow to simmer for 2–3 minutes. As the sauce cooks you'll see it change in colour and the sauce will begin to caramelise. Add the mango chutney, ground almonds, cashew butter, coconut flour, sugar, creamed coconut block and water, stirring well until the creamed coconut block is fully melted. Simmer for 2–3 minutes.

- Add the remaining curry broth, mix well and simmer for another 2–3 minutes until the sauce is slightly thick and bubbling hot. Add the fresh lemon juice or lemon dressing and mix once more. Pour the Ceylonese curry sauce into a long foil tray or serving dish, garnish with fresh coriander and serve with your favourite rice, bread and poppadoms.

TRADITIONAL AND STREET FOOD DISHES

The recipes included in this chapter fall between traditional Indian style and Indian street-food style. While there's absolutely nothing wrong with leftover takeaway-style curry for breakfast, traditional dishes such as Akoori (lightly spiced scrambled eggs with onion, tomato and green chillies) and Aloo Sabzi (potatoes in a mild gravy) are more authentic and make for a deliciously spicy start to the day.

Also included are a selection of mild and creamy dal dishes, as well as some street food favourites such as Disco Fry Egg and Chole, an aromatic chickpea dish.

KEEMA MATTAR (TRADITIONAL INDIAN STYLE)

Served alongside Aloo Jeera (page 154), this dish could very well be described as Indian mince and potatoes! If you have any leftover keema, use it to make Lamb Samosas (page 44) or mash the peas roughly with a fork and use the spicy keema mix to make stuffed Paratha Bread (page 172).

Serves 4

1 teaspoon cumin powder
½ teaspoon coriander powder
½ teaspoon turmeric
¼ teaspoon cinnamon powder
½ teaspoon garam masala
Pinch of Kashmiri red chilli powder
1 teaspoon dried fenugreek leaves (methi)
1 teaspoon caster sugar
½ teaspoon sea salt
Pinch of ground black pepper
2 teaspoons vegetable oil
1 onion, finely chopped
1 teaspoon Garlic Ginger Paste (page 228)
1 fresh green finger chilli, thinly sliced
500g lamb mince
120ml tomato passata
50ml water
1 bay leaf

125g frozen green peas
1 tablespoon fresh lemon juice or lemon dressing
Aloo Jeera (page 154) or Plain Basmati Rice (page 186), to
   serve

- Put the cumin powder, coriander powder, turmeric, cinnamon powder, garam masala, red chilli powder, dried fenugreek leaves, sugar, sea salt and black pepper in a bowl. Mix and set aside.

- Heat the oil in a large pan over a medium to high heat, add the chopped onion and stir-fry for 2–3 minutes until the onion begins to soften. Add the garlic ginger paste and green chilli and cook for a further 30 seconds. Add the lamb mince and cook, stirring often, for 2–3 minutes or until the mince is evenly browned. Drain off any excess fat if desired.

- Add the prepared spices and mix well. Cook for about 1 minute or until the raw aroma of the spices cooks out, then add the tomato passata, water and bay leaf. Bring to the boil, reduce the heat to low and simmer for about 30 minutes, stirring occasionally. Add a little water as the mince cooks if you feel the sauce is becoming too dry.

- Add the frozen peas, mix well and simmer for a further 5–6 minutes. Remove the bay leaf. Finish the keema with the fresh lemon juice or lemon dressing and serve with aloo jeera or plain rice.

CHANA ALOO MASALA
(TRADITIONAL INDIAN STYLE)

This simple chickpea and potato dish is full of fragrant spices – I love eating this cold for breakfast!

Serves 2

250g new potatoes
2 teaspoons cumin powder
1 teaspoon coriander powder
1 teaspoon garam masala
1 teaspoon turmeric
Pinch of Kashmiri red chilli powder
1 teaspoon dried fenugreek leaves (methi)
¼ teaspoon sea salt, plus a pinch for the potatoes
150ml water, plus 2 tablespoons for the spice mix
1 tablespoon vegetable oil
1 medium onion, finely chopped
2 teaspoons Garlic Ginger Paste (page 228)
1 fresh green finger chilli, thinly sliced
150g crushed tomatoes or passata
400g tin chickpeas, drained and rinsed
1 tablespoon fresh lemon juice or lemon dressing
1 small handful fresh coriander leaves, finely chopped
Plain Chapatis (page 170) or Poppadoms (page 215), to
    serve

- Put the potatoes in a pan, cover with water, add a pinch of salt and boil for 10–12 minutes or until the potatoes are just turning soft. Drain and set aside.

- Put the cumin powder, coriander powder, garam masala, turmeric, red chilli powder, dried fenugreek leaves and sea salt in a bowl. Add the 2 tablespoons of water, mix well and set aside.

- Heat the vegetable oil in a curry pan or frying pan over a medium heat. Add the chopped onion and fry for 5 minutes, stirring often until the onions are soft, then add the garlic ginger paste and green chilli and fry for a further 1 minute.

- Add the prepared spices in water, mix well and cook the spices for about 1 minute until the raw aroma disappears. Add the crushed tomatoes or passata, drained chickpeas and 150ml water and mix well once more. Add the parboiled new potatoes and mix well. Bring to the boil, reduce the heat to low and simmer for about 15 minutes until the sauce just begins to thicken.

- Finish the curry with fresh lemon juice or lemon dressing and fresh coriander leaves. Serve with plain chapatis or poppadoms.

RED LENTIL & POTATO CURRY
(TRADITIONAL INDIAN STYLE)

Serves 4–6

2 teaspoons cumin powder
1 teaspoon coriander powder
1 teaspoon garam masala
1 teaspoon turmeric
Pinch of Kashmiri red chilli powder
1 teaspoon dried fenugreek leaves (methi)
¼ teaspoon sea salt
1 tablespoon vegetable oil
1 medium onion, finely chopped
2 teaspoons Garlic Ginger Paste (page 228)
1 fresh green chilli, thinly sliced
150g crushed tomatoes or passata
150g red lentils, rinsed and drained
500ml water, plus 2 tablespoons for the spice mix
4–6 small new potatoes
1 tablespoon fresh lemon juice or lemon dressing
1 small handful fresh coriander leaves, finely chopped
Plain Chapatis (page 170) or Poppadoms (page 215), to serve

- Put the cumin powder, coriander powder, garam masala,
  turmeric, red chilli powder, dried fenugreek leaves and sea
  salt in a bowl. Add the 2 tablespoons of water, mix well and
  set aside.

- Heat the vegetable oil in a curry pan or frying pan over a medium heat, add the chopped onion and fry for 5 minutes, stirring often until the onion is soft. Add the garlic ginger paste and green chilli and fry for a further 1 minute.

- Add the prepared spices in water and mix well. Cook the spices for about 1 minute until the raw aroma disappears, then add the crushed tomatoes or passata, red lentils and 500ml water and mix well once more. Add the new potatoes, bring to the boil, reduce the heat to low and simmer for about 1 hour until the lentils are soft, the potatoes are cooked and the sauce is slightly thick. Stir the lentils from time to time, adding a little water if the lentils are thickening too quickly.

- Finish the curry with fresh lemon juice or lemon dressing and fresh coriander leaves. Serve with plain chapatis or poppadoms.

TARKA DAL (TRADITIONAL INDIAN STYLE)

This simple dal is warm and delicious, comfort food at its best. If desired, the red lentils may be cooked ahead of time and kept covered in the refrigerator until needed (up to 2 days).

Serves 1–2

100g red lentils, rinsed and drained
½ teaspoon turmeric
400ml water
1 teaspoon vegetable oil
¼ teaspoon sea salt
1 tablespoon ghee
½ teaspoon cumin seeds
½ teaspoon mustard seeds
2 whole dried red chillies, each cut into three pieces
1 small onion, finely chopped
2 teaspoons Garlic Ginger Paste (page 228)
1 fresh green finger chilli, thinly sliced
1 salad tomato, finely chopped
1 small handful fresh coriander leaves, finely chopped
Plain Basmati Rice (page 186) or Plain Chapatis (page 170), to serve

- Put the red lentils, turmeric, water and vegetable oil in a pan. Bring to the boil, reduce the heat to low and simmer for 30–40 minutes or until the lentils are soft. Stir the lentils often, adding a little water if the lentils are thickening too quickly. Set aside.

- Heat the ghee in a curry pan or frying pan over a medium heat, add the cumin seeds, mustard seeds, dried red chillies and chopped onion and fry for 3–4 minutes until the onion is soft and beginning to darken. Add the garlic ginger paste and sliced green chilli and fry for a further 30 seconds, then add the chopped tomato and mix well once more.

- Add the cooked dal to the curry pan or frying pan, mix thoroughly and simmer for 1–2 minutes until fully combined. Finish with fresh coriander leaves and serve with plain basmati rice or plain chapatis.

CHOLAR DAL (TRADITIONAL INDIAN STYLE)

This Bengali-style dal is slightly sweet with coconut and raisins.

Serves 1

- 100g chana dal (dried split chickpeas), washed 2–3 times until the water runs clear
- 225ml cold water
- ½ teaspoon yellow mustard seeds
- ½ teaspoon cumin seeds
- 2 cloves
- 2 green cardamom pods, crushed (seeds only)
- 2 whole dried red chillies, each cut into 3 pieces
- 1 tablespoon desiccated coconut, plus a little extra to serve
- Pinch of garam masala
- Pinch of cinnamon powder
- Pinch of Kashmiri red chilli powder
- ¼ teaspoon turmeric
- ¼ teaspoon sea salt
- ½ teaspoon caster sugar
- 1 tablespoon vegetable oil
- ½ teaspoon Garlic Ginger Paste (page 228)
- 1 tablespoon raisins, plus 2 or 3 extra to serve
- 1 teaspoon ghee
- Plain Chapatis (page 170), to serve

- Cover the washed chana dal with water and set aside for 1 hour 30 minutes.

- Drain the dal, tip it into a pan and cover with the fresh cold water. Bring to the boil, skimming off any impurities (foam) that rise to the top with a spoon. Reduce the heat to low and cook the dal for about 45 minutes, stirring often, until soft. Add a little water as the dal cooks if it becomes too dry. Set aside until needed.

- Put the yellow mustard seeds, cumin seeds, cloves, seeds from the crushed cardamom pods, dried red chillies and desiccated coconut in a bowl. In a separate bowl, place the garam masala, cinnamon powder, red chilli powder, turmeric, sea salt and sugar. Mix and set aside.

- Heat the vegetable oil in a curry pan or frying pan over a medium heat, add the prepared whole spices (mustard seeds, cumin seeds etc.) and stir-fry for 30 seconds, then add the garlic ginger paste, raisins, prepared ground spices (garam masala, cinnamon powder etc.) and stir-fry for a further 30 seconds, adding a splash of water if necessary, to prevent the spices from burning.

- Pour the cooked dal into the sizzling spices and mix thoroughly. Simmer the cholar dal for 1–2 minutes until piping hot, adding a splash of water if needed until the dal reaches the desired consistency (it should be slightly thick). Finish with the teaspoon of ghee, pour the cholar dal into a foil tray or serving dish, garnish with a little more desiccated coconut and raisins and serve with plain chapatis.

AKOORI, INDIAN SCRAMBLED EGGS
(TRADITIONAL INDIAN STYLE)

These lightly spiced eggs are utterly delicious alongside warm chapatis brushed generously with ghee.

Serves 1

Pinch of cumin powder
Pinch of garam masala
Pinch of turmeric
Pinch of sea salt
Pinch of ground black pepper
1 teaspoon vegetable oil
¼ onion, finely chopped
1 teaspoon Garlic Ginger Paste (page 228)
½ fresh green chilli, thinly sliced
½ salad tomato, finely chopped
2 eggs, whisked
1 small handful fresh coriander leaves, finely chopped
3 Plain Chapatis (page 170), generously brushed with
    ghee, to serve

- Put the cumin powder, garam masala, turmeric, sea salt and black pepper in a small bowl. Mix and set aside.

- Heat the vegetable oil in a pan over a medium heat, add the onion and stir-fry for 1 minute until it just begins to soften. Add the garlic ginger paste and sliced fresh green chilli and stir-fry for a further 30 seconds. Add the prepared spices and chopped tomato and stir-fry for 1 minute.

- Reduce the heat to low, add the whisked eggs and stir gently for 2–3 minutes until the eggs are scrambled. Add the fresh coriander leaves, mix once more and serve with the ghee-brushed chapatis.

ALOO SABZI (INDIAN STREET-FOOD STYLE)

This simple dish of potatoes in a curried gravy sauce is a popular Indian street food, served for breakfast alongside fried Puri Breads (page 174). I like to prepare and cook this in the evening, set it aside in the refrigerator to allow the flavours to be soaked up in the potatoes, then reheat it for breakfast the next day, adding a splash of water if necessary.

Serves 1–2

  3 medium new potatoes (about 300g), diced (you can peel
    them if desired, but I like to leave the skin on)
  ¼ teaspoon cumin powder
  Pinch of coriander powder
  ½ teaspoon Kashmiri red chilli powder
  ¼ teaspoon dried fenugreek leaves (methi)
  ¼ teaspoon turmeric
  ¼ teaspoon sea salt, plus a pinch for cooking the potatoes
  250ml water, plus 1 tablespoon for the spice mix
  2 tablespoons vegetable oil
  ½ teaspoon cumin seeds
  1 fresh green finger chilli, thinly sliced
  ¼ teaspoon garam masala
  1 tablespoon fresh lemon juice or lemon dressing
  1 small handful fresh coriander leaves, finely chopped
  Puri Breads (page 174) or lightly toasted Pav (page 179),
    to serve

- Fill a large pan with water, add a pinch of salt and the new potatoes. Bring to the boil and simmer for about 12 minutes or until the potatoes are almost completely soft. Drain and set aside to cool.

- Put the cumin powder, coriander powder, red chilli powder, dried fenugreek leaves, turmeric, sea salt and tablespoon of water in a small bowl. Mix well and set aside.

- Heat the vegetable oil in a curry pan or frying pan set over a medium heat, add the cumin seeds and sliced fresh green chilli and stir-fry for 30 seconds. Add the prepared spice mix and stir-fry for 1–2 minutes until the spices lose their raw aroma, then add the potatoes and 250ml water, bring to a simmer and cook over a low to medium heat for 10–12 minutes. If you prefer a slightly thicker gravy, crush some of the potatoes into the sauce as it simmers.

- Add the garam masala, fresh lemon juice or lemon dressing and fresh coriander leaves. Mix well, pour the aloo sabzi into a foil tray or onto a serving plate and serve with puri breads or lightly toasted pav.

CHOLE (INDIAN STREET-FOOD STYLE)

The use of black tea in this recipe may sound unusual but it brings great colour and a depth of flavour to the dish. Coupled with chaat masala in the spice mix, the resulting flavour is slightly fruity and utterly delicious.

Serves 2

1 green cardamom pod, crushed
¼ cinnamon stick or cassia bark
1 Indian bay leaf
3 cloves
¼ teaspoon cumin seeds
½ teaspoon garam masala
¼ teaspoon chaat masala
¼ teaspoon coriander powder
¼ teaspoon mild chilli powder
¼ teaspoon turmeric
1 teaspoon dried fenugreek leaves (methi)
¼ teaspoon sea salt
250ml water
1 English breakfast tea or other black tea bag
½ teaspoon brown sugar
1 generous tablespoon sunflower oil
1 medium red onion, finely chopped
1 teaspoon Garlic Ginger Paste (page 228)
1 fresh green finger chilli, finely chopped

2 teaspoons tomato purée mixed with 1 tablespoon water
400g tin chickpeas, drained and rinsed
1 small handful fresh coriander leaves, finely chopped
Puri Breads (page 174), to serve

- Put the crushed green cardamom, cinnamon stick, bay leaf, cloves and cumin seeds in a bowl. Mix and set aside. Put the garam masala, chaat masala, coriander powder, mild chilli powder, turmeric, dried fenugreek leaves and sea salt in another bowl. Mix briefly and set aside.

- Boil the water and brew the tea with the brown sugar for about 1 minute. Remove the tea bag and set the brewed tea aside.

- Heat the oil in a curry pan or frying pan over a medium heat, add the green cardamom, cinnamon stick, bay leaf, cloves and cumin seed mix and stir-fry for 30–40 seconds until the whole spices infuse the oil and it becomes aromatic. Add the chopped onion and stir-fry for 2–3 minutes or until the onion begins to soften, then add the garlic ginger paste, fresh green chilli and tomato purée mix and stir-fry for a further 2 minutes.

- Add the prepared ground spices (garam masala etc.) and stir-fry for 30-40 seconds until the spices become aromatic. Add a splash of water as necessary to ensure the spices don't burn. Add the drained chickpeas and the brewed tea, mix well, bring to the boil, reduce the heat to low and simmer for 10–12 minutes, stirring occasionally. Add a little extra water if the sauce begins to dry up too quickly. If a thicker gravy is required, use a fork to mash some of the chickpeas as the chole cooks.

- Finish the chole with the fresh coriander, mix once more and serve with puri breads.

EGG KHATI ROLLS (INDIAN STREET-FOOD STYLE)

These simple bread omelette wraps are delicious as described below, or can be stuffed with your favourite fillings, including Tandoori Chicken (page 48) and sliced onions or peppers.

Serves 2 (Makes 2 rolls)

100g chapati flour, plus extra for dusting
Pinch of sea salt
60–75ml cold water
2 teaspoons vegetable oil, plus extra for greasing
2 eggs
½ fresh green finger chilli, finely chopped
¼ teaspoon chaat masala
1 small handful fresh coriander leaves, finely chopped
Your favourite chutney, to serve

- Put the chapati flour and sea salt in a large bowl. Mix briefly. Slowly add the water, stirring until a dough begins to form. Add the vegetable oil and mix well.

- Tip the dough out onto a well-floured work surface and knead it for 2–3 minutes. Once the dough is smooth, form it into a ball and place it in a lightly oiled bowl. Cover with a clean, damp cloth and set aside for 30 minutes. After 30 minutes, the dough is ready to use. Alternatively, cover with cling film and set aside in the refrigerator for up to 24 hours.

- Put the eggs, fresh green chilli, chaat masala and fresh coriander in a bowl and whisk thoroughly.

- Heat a dry frying pan or tava pan over a medium heat. Divide the dough into 2 equal pieces, roll each into a ball and keep covered with a clean, damp cloth while you work. Lightly dust your work surface and rolling pin with flour. Working with one chapati at a time, roll out the dough into a 30cm circle. Carefully place the chapati on the preheated pan and cook for about 30 seconds. Use a spatula to flip the chapati over and cook for a further 30 seconds. As the chapati cooks you'll begin to see the colour change and small bubbles beginning to form.

- Lift the chapati out of the pan and add half of the whisked egg mix to the pan, swirling the pan in a circular motion to encourage the egg to cover the base. Return the chapati to the pan and use a spatula to press the bread down into the egg. Cook for 30–40 seconds or until the egg is set, flip the bread so that the egg layer is on top and remove from the pan. Repeat the process with the remaining chapati dough and egg mix.

- Roll the egg khati wraps and serve with your favourite chutney.

BOMBAY GRILLED SANDWICH
(INDIAN STREET-FOOD STYLE)

This generously filled 'toastie'-style sandwich is quite the combination of flavours. If you have a deep-fill toastie machine you can use that to cook this sandwich instead.

Serves 1

2 white or wholemeal bread slices
2 teaspoons salted butter
1 teaspoon Coriander Chutney (page 204)
1 teaspoon Mint Chutney (page 207)
3–4 tomato slices
3–4 cooked beetroot slices
3–4 cooked potato slices
3–4 cucumber slices
½ small red onion, finely chopped
1 small handful grated cheddar cheese (optional)
Pinch of sea salt or chaat masala
1 teaspoon vegetable oil
Ketchup and/or your favourite chutneys, to serve

- Spread the bread slices with ½ teaspoon each of salted butter, reserving the remaining butter. Add the coriander chutney on one slice of bread and mint chutney on the other. Layer one slice of bread with the sliced tomato, beetroot, potato and cucumber. Top with chopped onion and cheddar cheese (if desired) and season with sea salt or chaat masala. Add the remaining bread slice to form a sandwich.

- Heat a heavy frying pan or griddle pan over a medium heat. Add the vegetable oil and the remaining salted butter. Add the sandwich to the pan and cook for 3–4 minutes, or until the bottom of the sandwich is golden and crisp. Carefully flip the sandwich with a spatula and cook for a further 2–3 minutes until both sides are cooked to perfection. Remove the sandwich from the pan, slice into two triangles and serve with ketchup and/or your favourite chutneys.

VADA PAV (INDIAN STREET-FOOD STYLE)

Serves 2–4 (Makes 4 rolls)

2–3 new potatoes (about 200g), peeled
Pinch of sea salt
1 tablespoon vegetable oil
¼ teaspoon cumin seeds
¼ teaspoon yellow mustard seeds
1 teaspoon Garlic Ginger Paste (page 228)
1 fresh green finger chilli, thinly sliced
¼ teaspoon turmeric
1 teaspoon fresh lemon juice or lemon dressing
1 small handful fresh coriander leaves, finely chopped
2 fresh green finger chillies, sliced lengthways (seeds and
    pith removed, or keep them in if you like it hot!)
2 teaspoons ghee
4 soft white bread rolls (Pav, page 179), split in half

Pakora batter
75g gram flour (chickpea flour)
2 tablespoons rice flour
Pinch of cumin powder
¼ teaspoon garam masala
¼ teaspoon turmeric
¼ teaspoon Kashmiri red chilli powder
Pinch of dried fenugreek leaves (methi)
¼ teaspoon sea salt

Pinch of bicarbonate of soda
About 100ml cold water
Vegetable oil for deep-frying

To serve
Dry Garlic Coconut Chutney (page 206)
Coriander Chutney (page 204)
Tomato ketchup

- Put the potatoes in a pan, cover with water, add the pinch of salt, bring to the boil and cook for 15 minutes or until just soft. Drain and mash the potatoes roughly, then set aside.

- Heat the vegetable oil in a curry pan or frying pan over a medium heat, add the cumin seeds and yellow mustard seeds and stir-fry for 20 seconds. Add the garlic ginger paste, thinly sliced green chilli, turmeric, fresh lemon juice or lemon dressing and fresh coriander leaves. Mix well, add the mashed potatoes and mix thoroughly. Set aside to cool. At this stage you can carry on with the rest of the process, or cover and refrigerate the potato mix overnight. Chilling the potato mix overnight improves the flavour and helps ensure the mix stays together.

- To finish the vada pav, first make the batter. Put the gram flour, rice flour, cumin powder, garam masala, turmeric, red chilli powder, dried fenugreek leaves, sea salt and bicarbonate of soda in a bowl. Mix briefly, then slowly add the water, whisking thoroughly until you have a smooth and slightly thick batter.

- Heat the oil for deep-frying to 180°C/350°F. If you're using a deep-fat fryer with a basket, remove the basket before heating the oil (the pakoras would stick to the basket).

- Divide the potato mix into four pieces, shape each into a ball, dip each ball into the pakora batter and carefully place in the hot oil. Fry for 3–4 minutes, or until crisp and golden. Remove from the oil with a slotted spoon and set aside on a plate lined with kitchen paper.

- Dip the green chillies that have been sliced lengthways into the pakora batter and carefully place them in the hot oil. Fry the chilli pakoras for 2 minutes until golden. Set to one side, with the potato pakoras.

- Heat the ghee in a curry pan or frying pan over a medium heat. Toast the bread rolls in the pan, allowing each of them to soak up a little of the melted ghee. Fill each bread roll with the cooked potato pakoras and serve with the chilli pakoras and some dry coconut chutney, coriander chutney and ketchup.

DISCO FRY EGG (INDIAN STREET-FOOD STYLE)

Serves 1

2 teaspoons vegetable oil
½ onion, finely chopped
1–2 fresh green chillies, thinly sliced
1 small handful fresh coriander leaves, finely chopped
1 egg
2 pinches of garam masala
2 pinches of turmeric
2 pinches of Kashmiri red chilli powder
2 pinches of sea salt
1 bread roll (Pav, page 179)

- Heat half the vegetable oil in a curry pan or frying pan over a medium heat, add half of the chopped onion, green chillies and fresh coriander leaves and cook for a few seconds.

- Crack the egg into the pan on top of the onion, chillies and coriander, and immediately burst the yolk, encouraging it to spread a little with a spatula. Add 1 pinch of the garam masala, turmeric, red chilli powder and sea salt. Slice open the bread roll and press it face down into the mixture.

- Top the bread roll with the remaining oil and another pinch each of garam masala, turmeric, red chilli powder and sea salt. Press down with a spatula to encourage the bread and the egg to combine to create a spicy bread omelette. Cook the bread omelette for a further 2 minutes, flipping it occasionally until cooked and a little crispy.

- Arrange the disco fry egg on a serving plate and serve with the remaining chopped onion, green chillies and fresh coriander leaves.

INSTANT DOSAS (INDIAN STREET-FOOD STYLE)

Making an authentic Indian dosa with soaked and fermented dal and rice is a real labour of love and an art in itself. This simpler instant version makes up with ease and flavour what it lacks in tradition!

Serves 1

60g gram flour (chickpea flour)
20g rice flour
Pinch of cumin seeds
Pinch of turmeric
½ teaspoon sea salt
About 90ml cold water
1–2 teaspoons vegetable oil

To serve
Aloo Jeera (page 154)
Selection of chutneys

- Put the gram flour, rice flour, cumin seeds, turmeric and sea salt in a bowl. Mix briefly. Add the water and whisk until you have a smooth, slightly thick batter. Set aside for 10 minutes.

- Heat a non-stick frying pan or crepe pan over a medium heat. Pour half of the batter into the pan, swirling the pan to create a thin pancake. Dot the dosa pancake with about 1 teaspoon of oil as it cooks. Cook for about 1 minute, or until the sides of the dosa begin to lift away from the pan. Use a flat spatula to carefully release the dosa from the pan and either fold it twice to form the classic dosa shape, or flip and cook the other side for 30 seconds for a crispier dosa. Set aside on a plate and repeat the process with the remaining batter.

- Serve the instant dosas with aloo jeera, and a selection of your favourite chutneys.

SIDE DISHES

While a main curry dish is undoubtedly the lead in the story, the backup provided by co-stars such as Aloo Jeera and Saag Aloo cannot be understated. This chapter includes recipes for vegetable-based side dishes which will ensure your curry night becomes an entire feast for both you and your guests. Served up alongside your favourite curry sauces and breads, you'll quickly come to love these accompaniments.

ALOO JEERA (TRADITIONAL INDIAN STYLE)

Serves 2

4 medium new potatoes (200–250g), diced (I like to leave
  the skin on, but peel if you wish)
½ teaspoon cumin powder
Pinch of coriander powder
Pinch of turmeric
1 teaspoon Kashmiri red chilli powder
1 teaspoon dried fenugreek leaves (methi)
½ teaspoon sea salt, plus a pinch for the potatoes
1 teaspoon cumin seeds
½ teaspoon coriander seeds
1 teaspoon yellow mustard seeds
2 tablespoons ghee
½ teaspoon Garlic Ginger Paste (page 228)
1 fresh green finger chilli, thinly sliced
50ml water
1 tablespoon fresh lemon juice or lemon dressing
1 small handful fresh coriander leaves, finely
  chopped

- Fill a large pan with water and add a pinch of salt and the
  new potatoes. Bring to the boil and simmer for about 12
  minutes, or until the potatoes are almost completely soft.
  Drain and set aside to cool.

- Put the cumin powder, coriander powder, turmeric, red chilli powder, dried fenugreek leaves and sea salt in a small bowl, mix and set aside. Put the cumin seeds, coriander seeds and yellow mustard seeds in a separate small bowl, mix and set aside.

- Heat the ghee in a curry pan or frying pan set over a medium heat. Add the mixed cumin, coriander and yellow mustard seeds and stir-fry for 30 seconds, then add the garlic ginger paste and green chilli and stir-fry for a further 30 seconds. Add the other bowl of mixed spices, mix well and stir-fry for a further 30 seconds.

- Add the cooked potatoes to the pan and mix well. Add the water and simmer for 1–2 minutes. Add the fresh lemon juice or lemon dressing and fresh coriander leaves, mix once more and serve alongside your favourite curry dishes.

ALOO GOBI (TRADITIONAL INDIAN STYLE)

Serves 2

1 tablespoon vegetable oil

4 medium new potatoes (200–250g), diced (I like to leave the skin on, but peel if you wish)

1 small cauliflower, cut into bite-sized florets

1 small onion, finely chopped

2 teaspoons Garlic Ginger Paste (page 228)

½ teaspoon coriander powder

¼ teaspoon garam masala

¼ teaspoon Kashmiri red chilli powder

¼ teaspoon sea salt

3 tablespoons chopped tomatoes (from a tin)

3 tablespoons water

1 small handful fresh coriander leaves, finely chopped

1 tablespoon fresh lemon juice or lemon dressing

- Heat the vegetable oil in a large pan set over a medium heat, add the diced potatoes and stir-fry for 5–6 minutes, then add the cauliflower florets and stir-fry for a further 5–6 minutes. Remove the potato and cauliflower from the pan and set aside.

- If the pan looks too dry, add a little more vegetable oil. Add the chopped onion and stir-fry for 2–3 minutes until soft, then add the garlic ginger paste and stir-fry for a further

1 minute. Add the coriander powder, garam masala, red chilli powder, sea salt, chopped tomatoes and water. Return the potato and cauliflower to the pan, mix well, cover with a lid and cook over a low to medium heat for 10–12 minutes, or until the vegetables are soft and the liquid is absorbed. Add a touch more water if the pan dries up too quickly.

- Add the fresh coriander leaves and fresh lemon juice or lemon dressing, mix once more and serve the aloo gobi alongside your favourite curry dishes.

SAAG ALOO (TRADITIONAL INDIAN STYLE)

Serves 2

¼ teaspoon coriander powder
¼ teaspoon turmeric
¼ teaspoon Kashmiri red chilli powder
¼ teaspoon dried fenugreek leaves (methi)
¼ teaspoon sea salt
Pinch of ground black pepper
1 tablespoon water
½ teaspoon cumin seeds
½ teaspoon yellow mustard seeds
½ teaspoon black onion seeds (kalonji)
1 tablespoon vegetable oil
1 small onion, finely chopped
2 teaspoons Garlic Ginger Paste (page 228)
1 fresh green chilli, finely sliced
250g new potatoes, diced (about 4 small–medium potatoes)
75ml water
75g fresh baby spinach leaves, roughly chopped
¼ teaspoon garam masala

- Put the coriander powder, turmeric, red chilli powder, dried fenugreek leaves, sea salt, black pepper and 1 tablespoon of water in a bowl. Mix briefly and set aside. Put the cumin seeds, yellow mustard seeds and black onion seeds in a separate bowl. Mix and set aside.

- Heat the vegetable oil in a curry pan or frying pan over a medium heat, add the cumin seeds, yellow mustard seeds and black onion seeds and stir-fry for 20 seconds. Add the chopped onion and stir-fry for a further 5–6 minutes, or until the onion is soft, then add the garlic ginger paste and fresh green chilli and stir-fry for a further 2 minutes. Add the prepared ground spices (coriander powder, etc.) and stir-fry for a further 30 seconds.

- Add the diced potatoes and 75ml of water and simmer for about 12 minutes or until the potatoes are just soft. Add the spinach leaves and mix through for 1 minute until the spinach is wilted. Finish the saag aloo with the garam masala and serve alongside your favourite curry dishes.

MASALA FRIES (INDIAN STREET-FOOD STYLE)

Serves 2

½ teaspoon garam masala
¼ teaspoon chaat masala
¼ teaspoon mild chilli powder
¼ teaspoon sea salt
2 large floury potatoes (Maris Piper or King Edward),
    about 450g (skin on)
Vegetable oil for deep-frying
Garlic Sauce (page 213) or Mint Sauce (page 214), to serve

- Put the garam masala, chaat masala, chilli powder and sea salt in a bowl. Mix well.

- Slice the potatoes and cut into medium-thick chips. Put the potatoes in a bowl and cover with water. Set aside for 5 minutes. Drain the potatoes and rinse well with fresh water. Drain once more and use kitchen paper to dry the potato chips as much as possible.

- Heat the oil for deep-frying to about 150°C/300°F. Carefully add the chips to the oil and fry for 5–6 minutes, or until the chips are soft but not coloured. Remove from the oil with a slotted spoon and set aside on a plate to cool completely. At this stage the fries can be finished immediately, or alternatively cover and keep refrigerated for up to 24 hours.

- To finish the masala fries, heat the oil for deep-frying to about 180°C/350°F. Carefully add the chips to the oil and fry for 2–3 minutes, or until golden and crispy. Remove from the oil with a slotted spoon, place on a plate lined with kitchen paper to drain off any excess oil then place on a serving plate. Dust the chips generously with the prepared spices, toss to coat evenly and serve with garlic sauce or mint sauce.

CHANNA SUNDAL (TRADITIONAL INDIAN STYLE)

Serves 4 as a snack or side dish

A little sweet, a little spicy and a little savoury, this simple chickpea dish can be prepared in advance and served at room temperature, and it's perfect for snacking or serving alongside your favourite curry dishes.

1 teaspoon yellow mustard seeds
Pinch of cumin seeds
3 dried curry leaves
1 dried red chilli, cut into 3 pieces
1 tablespoon vegetable oil
1 fresh green finger chilli, thinly sliced
400g tin chickpeas, drained and rinsed
3 tablespoons desiccated coconut
Generous pinch of sea salt
Pinch of ground black pepper
1 tablespoon fresh lemon juice or lemon dressing
Pinch of garam masala
1 small handful fresh coriander leaves, finely chopped, to serve

- Put the yellow mustard seeds, cumin seeds, dried curry leaves and dried red chilli in a small bowl. Mix and set aside.

- Heat the vegetable oil in a curry pan or frying pan over a medium heat, add the bowl of whole spices and stir-fry for 30 seconds. Add the fresh green chilli and chickpeas and stir-fry for another 2 minutes.

- Switch off the heat and add the desiccated coconut. Mix well. Add the sea salt, black pepper, fresh lemon juice or lemon dressing and garam masala. Mix once more and pour the channa sundal into a foil tray or onto a serving plate. Garnish with fresh coriander leaves and serve warm or at room temperature.

SWEETCORN CHAAT (TRADITIONAL INDIAN STYLE)

Serves 2

¼ teaspoon Kashmiri red chilli powder

¼ teaspoon chaat masala

Generous pinch of sea salt

¼ teaspoon ground black pepper

2 teaspoons ghee

¼ teaspoon cumin seeds

280g tinned sweetcorn, drained and rinsed (drained weight)

1 small onion, finely chopped

1 salad tomato, finely chopped

1 teaspoon fresh lemon juice or lemon dressing

To serve

1 handful nylon sev

1 small handful fresh coriander leaves, finely chopped

- Put the red chilli powder, chaat masala, sea salt and black pepper in a small bowl. Mix and set aside.

- Heat the ghee in a pan over a medium heat. Add the cumin seeds and sweetcorn and stir-fry for 5–6 minutes, then add the mixed spices and stir-fry for a further 30 seconds. Remove the pan from the heat, add the chopped onion, salad tomato and fresh lemon juice or lemon dressing and mix well.

- Pour the sweetcorn chaat into a foil tray or serving dish and garnish with nylon sev and fresh coriander leaves just before serving.

ALOO CHANNA CHAAT (INDIAN STREET-FOOD STYLE)

This healthy snack is deliciously addictive – leftovers can be stored in the refrigerator and make for an easy breakfast dish the following day. For added indulgence, fry the potatoes instead of boiling them.

Serves 3–4 as a side dish or snack

4 small new potatoes, diced
¼ teaspoon chaat masala
Pinch of cumin powder
Pinch of Kashmiri red chilli powder
Pinch of mild chilli powder
Generous pinch of sea salt, plus an extra pinch for the potatoes
400g tin chickpeas, drained and rinsed
1 small red onion, finely chopped
1 fresh green finger chilli, thinly sliced
Dash of fresh lemon juice or lemon dressing
1 tablespoon Date & Tamarind Chutney (page 209)
1 small handful fresh coriander leaves, finely chopped, to serve

- Fill a large pan with water, add a pinch of salt and the new potatoes, bring to the boil and simmer for about 12 minutes or until the potatoes are almost soft. Drain and set aside.

- Put the chaat masala, cumin powder, red chilli powder, mild chilli powder and sea salt in a small bowl. Mix and set aside.

- Put the drained chickpeas in a large bowl. Add the cooked potatoes and the prepared bowl of spices. Add the red onion, fresh green chilli and fresh lemon juice or lemon dressing and mix well. Add the date and tamarind chutney and mix once more. Pour the aloo channa chaat into a foil tray or onto a serving plate, garnish with fresh coriander and serve.

CURRIED CHICKPEAS (INDIAN STREET-FOOD STYLE)

Spicy, salty and crunchy, these chickpeas are the perfect snack to appease your curry cravings! Use chaat masala instead of garam masala for a variation on the flavour.

Serves 2

1 teaspoon cumin powder
¼ teaspoon coriander powder
½ teaspoon garam masala
Pinch of mild red chilli powder
400g tin chickpeas, drained and rinsed
¼ teaspoon sea salt
1 tablespoon vegetable oil

- Preheat the oven to 180°C/Gas 4. Put the cumin powder, coriander powder, garam masala and mild chilli powder in a bowl. Mix and set aside.

- Pat the chickpeas dry with kitchen paper and spread them out on a roasting tray. Add the sea salt and vegetable oil and mix well. Roast the chickpeas for 15 minutes. Stir the chickpeas and roast for a further 15 minutes.

- Add the prepared spices to the chickpeas and mix well. Roast for another 10 minutes, or until crunchy. Set aside to cool completely before serving. The curried chickpeas will keep well in an airtight container for a couple of days.

INDIAN SPICED PEANUTS (INDIAN
STREET-FOOD STYLE)

Serves 4

150g unsalted peanuts
1 tablespoon vegetable oil
1 teaspoon garam masala
¼ teaspoon chaat masala
¼ teaspoon Kashmiri red chilli powder
Pinch of ground ginger
Pinch of cinnamon powder
1 tablespoon soft dark brown sugar
Pinch of sea salt

- Preheat the oven to 180°C/Gas 4. Put the peanuts, vegetable oil, garam masala, chaat masala, red chilli powder, ground ginger, cinnamon powder, dark brown sugar and sea salt in a bowl. Mix well.

- Pour the spiced nuts evenly onto a roasting tray and bake for 12–15 minutes until golden and toasted. Set aside to cool completely before serving. The spiced nuts will keep well in an airtight container for a couple of days.

BREADS

When you've put the time and effort into creating deliciously spicy, sweet and savoury curry sauces, it's only fitting that you have some good breads on the side to mop up every last drop. This chapter includes recipes for the various breads you'll commonly find at your favourite Indian takeaway restaurant.

Of course, some menu items such as naan breads are traditionally cooked in a tandoor oven. This clay-lined oven reaches incredibly high temperatures and the resultant skewers of meat and well-fired breads are quite something to behold. Luckily, with a few tricks and techniques, you can replicate the cooking process with a regular domestic oven and hob-top and achieve favourable results.

Other breads such as chapatis, parathas and fried puri breads can be more faithfully recreated, using exactly the same ingredients and techniques your local takeaway chef might use. These freshly made breads will soon become an integral part of your homemade curry experience!

PLAIN CHAPATIS (INDIAN RESTAURANT STYLE)

Serves 2 (Makes 6 small chapatis)

150g chapati flour, plus extra for dusting
Pinch of sea salt
80–100ml warm water
½ teaspoon vegetable oil, plus extra for greasing
1–2 teaspoons melted ghee or salted butter, to finish

- Put the chapati flour and sea salt in a large bowl. Mix briefly. Slowly add the water, stirring until a dough begins to form. Add the vegetable oil and mix once more.

- Tip the dough out onto a well-floured work surface and knead it for 3–4 minutes. Once the dough is smooth, form it into a ball and place it in a lightly oiled bowl. Cover with a clean, damp cloth and set aside for 30 minutes. The dough is now ready to use. Alternatively, cover with cling film and set aside in the refrigerator for up to 24 hours.

- To make the chapatis, heat a dry frying pan or tava pan over a medium heat. Divide the dough into 6 equal pieces, form each into a ball and keep covered with a clean, damp cloth while you work. Lightly dust your work surface and rolling pin with flour. Working with one chapati at a time, roll out the dough into a 15cm circle. Carefully place the chapati on the preheated pan and cook for about 30 seconds. Use a spatula to flip the chapati over and cook for a further

30 seconds. As the chapati cooks you'll see the colour begin to change and small bubbles beginning to form.

- Flip the chapati once more and press down gently with a clean cloth or spatula. The chapati should begin to puff up. At this stage the chapati is almost fully cooked and can be finished with a kitchen blow torch or directly on the flame of a gas hob to encourage the chapati to balloon, and to char the outsides nicely.

- Transfer the cooked chapati to a plate, brush with a little ghee or butter and cover with a clean tea towel to keep warm while you cook the rest of the chapatis. Serve with your favourite curry dishes.

THE INDIAN TAKEAWAY SECRET

PARATHA BREAD (INDIAN RESTAURANT STYLE)

Serves 2 (Makes 4 paratha breads)

150g chapati flour, plus extra for dusting
Pinch of sea salt
80–100ml warm water
½ teaspoon vegetable oil, plus extra for greasing
1–2 teaspoons melted ghee or vegetable oil

- Put the chapati flour and sea salt in a large bowl. Mix briefly. Slowly add the water, stirring until a dough begins to form. Add the vegetable oil and mix once more.

- Tip the dough out onto a well-floured work surface and knead it for 3–4 minutes. Once the dough is smooth, form it into a ball and place it in a lightly oiled bowl. Cover with a clean, damp cloth and set aside for 30 minutes. The dough is now ready to use. Alternatively, cover with cling film and set aside in the refrigerator for up to 24 hours.

- Divide the dough into 4 equal pieces and form each piece of dough into a ball. Working with one paratha at a time on a floured surface, roll out the dough into a 20cm circle.

- Brush the rolled-out paratha dough with a little melted ghee or vegetable oil. Roll the bread up like a sausage and, using floured hands, form it into a dough ball once again. Roll out the dough again into a circle. This creates a layer of fat within the dough similar to that made when preparing puff pastry.

- Heat a dry frying pan or tava pan over a medium heat. Carefully place the prepared paratha bread on the pan and cook the bread for about 2 minutes, turning it occasionally and brushing it with a little ghee or vegetable oil until the bread is golden and crispy, with some charring. Set aside and keep covered with a clean tea towel while you repeat the process with the remaining paratha breads.

- Serve the paratha breads with your favourite curry dishes.

Variation

To make stuffed parathas, add a tablespoon of leftover Vegetable Samosa filling (page 41) or Keema Mattar (page 124) to each circle of dough after rolling it out a second time. Form the dough into a ball again and roll the stuffed dough out once more before cooking as described above

PURI BREADS (INDIAN RESTAURANT STYLE)

These breads are surprisingly light, despite being fried in oil.

Serves 2 (Makes 6 small puri breads)

150g chapati flour, plus extra for dusting
Pinch of sea salt
80–100ml warm water
½ teaspoon vegetable oil, plus extra for greasing
Vegetable oil for deep-frying
Aloo Sabzi (page 136), to serve (optional)

- Put the chapati flour and sea salt in a large bowl. Mix briefly. Slowly add the water, stirring until a dough begins to form. Add the vegetable oil and mix once more.

- Tip the dough out onto a well-floured work surface and knead it for 3–4 minutes, adding just a little more chapati flour if necessary to prevent the dough from sticking. Once the dough is smooth, form it into a ball and place it in a lightly oiled bowl. Cover with a clean, damp cloth and set aside for 30 minutes. At this stage the dough is ready to use. Alternatively, cover with cling film and set aside in the refrigerator for up to 24 hours.

- To make the puris, heat the oil for deep-frying to about 180°C/350°F. Divide the dough into 6 equal pieces, form each into a ball and keep covered with a clean, damp cloth while you work. Lightly oil your work surface and rolling pin. Working with one puri bread at a time, roll out the dough into a 15cm circle. Carefully place the rolled-out dough into the hot oil and use a spoon to pour hot oil over the top of the puri bread – it will begin to balloon and puff up immediately. Fry for about 30 seconds, or until golden and coloured on the bottom, then carefully flip and fry for a further 20–30 seconds on the other side. Use a slotted spoon to remove the cooked puri bread from the pan and set aside on a plate lined with kitchen paper to soak up any excess oil.

- Repeat the process with the remaining dough until all 6 puri breads have been fried. Serve with aloo sabzi or alongside your favourite curry dishes.

NAAN BREADS (INDIAN RESTAURANT STYLE)

Serves 4 (Makes 4 naan breads)

300g strong white bread flour, plus extra for dusting
1 x 7g sachet of fast-action dried yeast
5 tablespoons natural yogurt
1 tablespoon vegetable oil, plus extra for greasing
125ml cold whole milk
1 teaspoon sea salt
2 tablespoons black onion seeds (kalonji) (optional)
1–2 tablespoons ghee or melted butter

- Put the bread flour and yeast in a large bowl. Mix well. Add the natural yogurt, vegetable oil and half the milk. Mix briefly until the ingredients are combined and set aside for 5 minutes. Alternatively, combine the ingredients in a stand mixer with a dough hook attached.

- Add the sea salt and the black onion seeds (if desired) to the dough. Mix well and slowly add the remaining milk until you have a soft dough. Tip the dough out onto a lightly floured work surface and knead it for 3–4 minutes, adding just a little more flour as necessary until the dough becomes smooth. Shape the dough into a ball.

- Lightly oil the bowl and return the dough to the bowl. Cover with a clean, damp cloth and leave to rise at room temperature for about 1 hour or until almost doubled in size.

- Knock the air out of the risen dough and divide it into 4 equal pieces. Roll each piece of dough out on a lightly floured work surface into the classic teardrop shape, no larger than your frying pan.

- Heat a dry, heavy cast-iron frying pan over a high heat until smoking. Put the naan bread dough in the pan and cook for 30 seconds, then move the naan bread a little to encourage even browning. Cook for a further 1 minute.

- Flip the naan bread over and continue to cook on the other side for a further 1–2 minutes or until cooked through. Alternatively, finish the naan bread underneath a very hot grill for 1–2 minutes.

- Remove the naan bread from the pan and arrange on a plate. Brush with ghee or melted butter and cover with foil or greaseproof paper to keep warm while you cook the rest of the naan breads.

- Serve the naan breads with your favourite curry dishes.

Variations
Garlic and Coriander Naan – In a bowl, mix 2 tablespoons of ghee or softened butter, 2 teaspoons of garlic powder and a pinch of fresh coriander leaves, finely chopped. Brush the cooked naan breads with the garlic and coriander butter.

Peshawari Naan – Put 2 tablespoons shelled pistachios, 2 tablespoons desiccated coconut and 2 tablespoons raisins in a blender. Blitz well. Add a tablespoon of the blended mixture to each piece of flattened dough. Form a ball again and roll the stuffed dough out once more before cooking as described above.

PAV (INDIAN STREET-FOOD STYLE)

These soft bread rolls are ideal for mopping up curry and are an essential part of Vada Pav (page 145).

Serves 3 (Makes 6 small rolls)

200g plain flour
½ teaspoon caster sugar
½ teaspoon sea salt
1 generous teaspoon fast-action dried yeast
2–3 tablespoons whole milk, plus extra for brushing
100ml cold water
1 teaspoon vegetable oil, for greasing
1 tablespoon salted butter, melted

- Put the plain flour, sugar, sea salt, yeast, milk and water in a stand mixer with a dough hook attached. Mix on medium speed for 5 minutes, or until a smooth dough is formed and the dough is coming away from the sides of the mixing bowl. Alternatively, mix and knead by hand to form a smooth dough.

- Lightly oil a bowl, put the dough in the bowl and cover with a clean, damp cloth. Set aside at room temperature for 1 hour 30 minutes.

- Knead the dough again and divide it into 6 equal pieces. Form each piece into a smooth ball. Lightly oil a baking tray and arrange the dough balls on the tray, leaving a little space between each for rising. Cover with lightly oiled cling film and set aside at room temperature for about 30 minutes, during which time the dough will rise further.

- Preheat the oven to 200°C/Gas 6. Brush the top of each dough ball with a little milk and bake the rolls for about 15 minutes, or until golden and hollow when tapped underneath. Remove the pav from the oven, brush with a little melted butter and serve warm, or set aside to cool completely on a wire rack.

- To toast your pav, heat a crepe pan or tava pan over a medium heat. Slice open the pav and add it to the pan. Add 1 teaspoon ghee and, as the ghee melts, use tongs to rub the pav through the melting ghee on both sides. Cook until warm and serve with your favourite curry dishes.

GARLIC CHILLI CHEESE TOASTS
(INDIAN STREET-FOOD STYLE)

Serves 2

2 tablespoons salted butter
1 teaspoon garlic powder
Pinch of dried parsley
Pinch of sea salt
Pinch of ground black pepper
2 white bread slices
50g mild or medium cheddar cheese, grated
50g mozzarella cheese, grated
2 fresh green finger chillies, thinly sliced (seeds and pith
    removed, or keep them in if you like it hot!)

- Put the salted butter, garlic powder, dried parsley, sea salt
  and black pepper in a bowl. Mix thoroughly to make a
  garlic butter.

- Heat the grill to medium-high. Lightly toast the bread
  slices under the grill until just a little golden on each side.
  Brush each toasted bread slice generously with the
  prepared garlic butter. Top with grated cheddar cheese
  and mozzarella cheese, add the sliced green chillies and
  place under the grill again until the cheese has melted. Cut
  the chilli cheese toasts into triangles and serve.

NOMI'S TANDOORI CHICKEN PIZZA
(INDIAN RESTAURANT STYLE)

Customers at Shezan who were in the know made sure to ask for one of Nomi's pizzas, a secret menu item from one of the most well-known takeaways in the south side of Glasgow.

Makes enough dough and sauce for 2 pizzas (both the dough and sauce can be frozen)

Dough
325g strong white bread flour, plus extra for dusting
½ teaspoon fast-action dried yeast
¾ teaspoon caster sugar
1 heaped teaspoon sea salt
200ml cold water
1 teaspoon olive oil
½ teaspoon vegetable oil, plus extra for greasing

Sauce
100g crushed tomatoes or passata
Pinch of garlic powder
Pinch of dried chilli flakes
Pinch of dried oregano
Pinch of sea salt
Pinch of ground black pepper
½ teaspoon olive oil

Per pizza

100g mozzarella cheese, grated

½ portion Tandoori Chicken Kebab, cooked and cooled (page 50)

¼ red onion, thinly sliced

¼ green pepper, thinly sliced

1 fresh green finger chilli, thinly sliced

2 tablespoons tinned sweetcorn, rinsed and drained

To serve (per pizza)

Pinch of dried oregano

Pinch of black pepper

- Put the white bread flour, yeast, caster sugar, sea salt and water in a stand mixer with a dough hook attached. Mix on medium speed for 1 minute until all of the water has been absorbed. Add the olive oil and vegetable oil and mix well at the same speed setting for 2–3 minutes until a smooth dough is formed. Alternatively, mix and knead by hand to form a smooth dough.

- Lightly oil two bowls. Divide the dough into two equal pieces and place one in each bowl. Cover the bowls with cling film and set aside in the refrigerator for 24 hours or up to 48 hours.

- To make the sauce, put the crushed tomatoes, garlic powder, dried chilli flakes, dried oregano, sea salt, black pepper and olive oil in a bowl. Mix well, cover and set aside in the refrigerator for up to 2 days.

- Remove the pizza dough from the fridge 1 hour before baking, remove the dough from the bowls and shape the dough into balls, keeping as much air in the dough as possible. Cover with lightly oiled cling film.

- Preheat a pizza stone in the oven at 240°C/Gas 9 for about 1 hour, and lightly oil a pizza tray.

- Dust one of the dough balls with a generous amount of flour and press out the dough by hand to form a 25–30cm circle. Arrange the dough on the lightly oiled pizza tray. Top the pizza with 3–4 tablespoons of the prepared pizza sauce. Add the grated mozzarella cheese, tandoori chicken, red onion, green pepper, green chilli and sweetcorn.

- Put the pizza (and the tray it's on) on top of the preheated pizza stone. Bake for 3 minutes. Give the pizza a shake and it should easily slide off the tray – slide the pizza directly onto the stone and bake for a further 3–4 minutes, rotating the pizza on the stone once or twice during this time to ensure the base browns evenly.

- Remove the pizza from the oven, garnish with a little dried oregano and black pepper, slice and serve.

- Repeat the process with the remaining dough, or freeze for use another day.

RICE

The fragrant aroma of good-quality basmati rice is noticeable as soon as the packet is opened and can be appreciated without any added ingredients, providing the rice is cooked well. Rice can vary greatly in quality and often contains a high level of starch, which needs to be properly washed out of the rice. Failure to do this thoroughly can result in stodgy, sticky rice. I've included a foolproof method for washing and cooking basmati rice which will deliver perfect results every time, with each individual grain of rice visible and separate from its friends.

Indian restaurants typically use food colourings to decorate the cooked rice – should you choose to do this, simply dot the cooked rice with a little colouring and let stand for 1–2 minutes before mixing through. I prefer not to use artificial colourings in my rice dishes, but this optional step may take you closer to the authentic takeaway restaurant experience.

Leftover cooked rice can be covered and stored for use the next day, providing it has been cooled down and refrigerated quickly. Use leftover rice for fried rice or biryani dishes the following day.

PLAIN BASMATI RICE (INDIAN RESTAURANT STYLE)

This basic rice cooking method is foolproof and provides guaranteed good results every time, providing the rice is washed until the water is clear and the rice-to-water ratio is followed. To make bigger portions, simply increase the quantity of rice and water, sticking to the ratio of one part rice to two parts water.

Serves 1–2

125g basmati rice
250ml water

- Put the basmati rice in a large bowl and cover completely with water. Mix briefly and set aside for 10 minutes. Drain the cloudy water, replace with fresh water and set aside again. Repeat this step once or twice more until the water is clear. Pour the rice into a sieve, rinse once more with fresh water and drain completely.

- Transfer the drained rice to a saucepan and cover with the 250ml of fresh water. Bring to the boil over a high heat, then as soon as the rice begins to boil, reduce the heat to the lowest setting, cover with a lid and cook for 14 minutes. After this time, switch off the heat, set the rice aside and allow to sit, untouched and with the lid still on, for a further 10 minutes. Fluff up the rice with a fork and serve with your favourite curry dishes.

- Alternatively, for fried rice, spread the rice out on a plate so it cools quickly, transfer to another plate, cover and set aside in the refrigerator overnight.

CUMIN RICE (INDIAN RESTAURANT STYLE)

Serves 2

> 125g basmati rice
> 1 teaspoon ghee
> ½ teaspoon cumin seeds
> 250ml water

- Put the basmati rice in a large bowl and cover completely with water. Mix briefly and set aside for 10 minutes. Drain the cloudy water, replace with fresh water and set aside again. Repeat this step once or twice more until the water is clear. Pour the rice into a sieve, rinse once more with fresh water and drain completely.

- Heat the ghee in a saucepan over a medium heat, add the cumin seeds and stir-fry for 20 seconds.

- Add the washed and drained rice and the 250ml of fresh water. Bring to the boil over a high heat and as soon as the rice begins to boil, reduce the heat to the lowest setting, cover with a lid and cook for 14 minutes. After this time, switch off the heat, set the rice aside and allow to sit, untouched and with the lid still on, for a further 10 minutes. Fluff up the rice with a fork and serve with your favourite curry dishes.

PILAU RICE (INDIAN RESTAURANT STYLE)

This fragrant rice is perfect alongside Tarka Dal (page 130).

Serves 2

125g basmati rice
2 teaspoons ghee
½ teaspoon cumin seeds
Seeds from 3 crushed green cardamom pods
2 cloves
Pinch of turmeric
250ml water
¼ cinnamon stick

- Put the basmati rice in a large bowl and cover completely with water. Mix briefly and set aside for 10 minutes. Drain the cloudy water, replace with fresh water and set aside again. Repeat this step once or twice more until the water is clear. Pour the rice into a sieve, rinse once more with fresh water and drain completely.

- Heat the ghee in a saucepan over a medium heat. Add the cumin seeds, cardamom seeds, cloves and turmeric and stir-fry for 20–30 seconds.

- Add the washed and drained rice and 250ml of fresh water then add the cinnamon stick. Bring to the boil over a high heat. As soon as the rice begins to boil, reduce the heat to the lowest setting, cover with a lid and cook for 14 minutes. After this time, switch off the heat, set the rice aside and allow to sit, untouched and with the lid still on, for a further 10 minutes. Fluff up the rice with a fork, remove the whole spices and serve with your favourite curry dishes.

FRIED RICE (INDIAN RESTAURANT STYLE)

Serves 2

2 teaspoons vegetable oil

½ small onion, finely chopped

¼ teaspoon Garlic Ginger Paste (page 228)

¼ teaspoon dried fenugreek leaves (methi)

Pinch of sea salt

½ teaspoon Madras curry powder

1 portion Plain Basmati Rice (page 186), cooled and
  refrigerated overnight

- Heat the vegetable oil in a curry pan or frying pan over a medium heat, add the chopped onion, garlic ginger paste, dried fenugreek leaves and sea salt and stir-fry for 1 minute.

- Add the Madras curry powder and basmati rice to the pan and mix well. Stir-fry for 2–3 minutes, then increase the heat to high and stir-fry for a further 30 seconds or until the rice is piping hot. Serve with your favourite curry dishes.

Variations

Mushroom Rice – Add 5–6 small button mushrooms, sliced, at the frying stage with the onion mixture.

Mixed Vegetable Rice – Add 4 tablespoons defrosted frozen mixed vegetables (broccoli, cauliflower, carrots, peas) at the frying stage with the onion mixture.

BIRYANI (INDIAN RESTAURANT STYLE)

While traditional Indian biryani dishes are a real labour of love, layered with flavour and a host of fragrant (and in the case of saffron, expensive!) spices, Indian restaurant biryani dishes in Scotland and the UK are typically a simpler affair, delicious nonetheless.

Serves 1–2

100–125ml Curry Broth (page 68 or page 72)
½ teaspoon Garlic Ginger Paste (page 228)
½ teaspoon tomato purée
Pinch of Kashmiri red chilli powder
¼ teaspoon dried fenugreek leaves (methi)
¼ teaspoon beetroot powder (optional, for colour)
Pinch of sea salt
1 small handful fresh coriander leaves, finely chopped
Cooked meat/vegetables as desired
1 portion Plain Basmati Rice (page 186), cooled and
    refrigerated overnight
Small pinch of fresh coriander leaves, finely chopped,
    to serve

- Heat 4 tablespoons of the curry broth in a curry pan or frying pan over a low to medium heat. Once the curry broth begins to sizzle, add the garlic ginger paste, tomato purée, red chilli powder, dried fenugreek leaves, beetroot powder (if desired), sea salt and chopped fresh coriander leaves. Mix well and simmer for 1–2 minutes.

- Add the cooked meat/vegetables as desired and about half of the remaining curry broth, mix well and allow to simmer for 2–3 minutes. As the sauce cooks you'll see it change in colour and the sauce will begin to caramelise.

- Add the remaining curry broth, mix once more and simmer for another 2–3 minutes until the sauce is thick. Add the cold rice, mix well and stir-fry for 2–3 minutes or until the rice is hot. Transfer the cooked biryani to a foil tray or serving dish, garnish with a little more chopped fresh coriander and serve with your favourite curry sauce on the side.

Note

Made using cooked basmati rice and a touch of curry sauce, restaurant-style biryani is an ideal way to use up leftovers from your curry night. Simply cool and store Plain Basmati Rice (page 186) or Cumin Rice (page 188) and any leftover curry in the refrigerator and combine stir-fry style – as described above – the following day.

SUNDRIES AND CHUTNEYS

If you've ever excitedly opened up your takeaway delivery only to feel the soul-crushing disappointment of the pakora sauce being forgotten in your order, you'll know only too well just how important add-ons are to a proper, full-on curry experience. Pakoras are nothing without the tangy pink pakora sauce, and poppadoms are missing a partner without fresh spiced onions on top. Fragrant and spicy seekh kebabs are the yin to the cooling mint sauce's yang.

This chapter includes recipes for all of the essential sides and chutneys you need to accompany your meal – spicy red chilli sauce, dry coconut chutney, cooling raita and mint sauce and, of course, the aforementioned spiced onions and pakora sauces. These menu items can be prepared ahead of time and will in fact benefit from an hour or two (or even a day or so) in the refrigerator, leaving you free to get on with cooking the starter dishes and main courses for your curry feast. All the kebab sauces and chutneys can be scaled up as desired if you have a lot of hungry guests to feed (or if you have a particular favourite that you just can't get enough of!).

At least this time, if the pakora sauce is forgotten, all that's required is a trip to the refrigerator!

SPICED ONIONS (INDIAN RESTAURANT STYLE)

The fresh and spicy flavour of these onions, combined with crisp Poppadoms (page 215), is the ultimate way to begin (or end!) an Indian restaurant-style meal.

Serves 2–4

2 medium-large onions, finely chopped
4 tablespoons tomato ketchup
1 teaspoon mint sauce
1 teaspoon mango chutney
Pinch of cumin powder
Pinch of garam masala
¼ teaspoon mild red chilli powder
¼ teaspoon beetroot powder (optional, for colour)
Pinch of sea salt
2 tablespoons water

- Put the onions in a large bowl, cover completely with cold water and set aside for 5 minutes. Drain through a sieve and return the chopped onions to a dry bowl.

- Add the tomato ketchup, mint sauce, mango chutney, cumin powder, garam masala, red chilli powder, beetroot powder (if desired), sea salt and water. Mix well, allow to stand for 5 minutes, mix once more and transfer the spiced onions to an airtight container.

- Cover and set aside in the refrigerator for at least 1 hour before serving with crispy poppadoms.

- The prepared spiced onions will keep well in the refrigerator for up to 2 days.

SPICED ONION SALAD (INDIAN TAKEAWAY STYLE)

On the beautiful Island of Arran, the only Indian takeaway in town serves up a spiced onion salad very similar to this one to happy locals and tourists alike.

Serves 4

2 medium-large onions, thinly sliced
1 salad tomato, thinly sliced
1 small handful shredded iceberg lettuce
¼ cucumber, peeled, deseeded and thinly sliced
2 tablespoons tomato ketchup
1 teaspoon mint sauce
1 teaspoon mango chutney
Pinch of cumin powder
Pinch of garam masala
¼ teaspoon mild red chilli powder
¼ teaspoon beetroot powder (optional, for colour)
Pinch of sea salt
1 teaspoon fresh lemon juice or lemon dressing

- Put the sliced onions, tomato, iceberg lettuce and cucumber in a bowl. Mix well. Add the tomato ketchup, mint sauce, mango chutney, cumin powder, garam masala, red chilli powder, beetroot powder (if desired), sea salt and fresh lemon juice or lemon dressing.

- Mix thoroughly once more, transfer the salad to an airtight container, cover and set aside in the refrigerator for 1 hour before serving.

ONION & CORIANDER SALAD
(INDIAN RESTAURANT STYLE)

Serves 2

1 large red onion, very thinly sliced
2 salad tomatoes, deseeded and chopped
Pinch of sea salt
¼ teaspoon Kashmiri red chilli powder
1 tablespoon fresh lemon juice or lemon dressing
Pinch of beetroot powder (optional, for colour)
1 small handful fresh coriander leaves, finely chopped

- Put the thinly sliced onion, chopped tomatoes, sea salt, red chilli powder, fresh lemon juice or lemon dressing and beetroot powder (if desired) in a bowl. Mix well and set aside in the refrigerator for 30 minutes.

- Garnish the onion salad with fresh coriander leaves just before serving.

CARROT & CASHEW SALAD
(TRADITIONAL INDIAN STYLE)

Serves 1–2

1 tablespoon raw cashews
2 large carrots, peeled and grated
1 fresh green finger chilli, thinly sliced
1 small handful fresh coriander leaves, finely chopped
2 teaspoons vegetable oil
¼ teaspoon cumin seeds
Pinch of turmeric
Pinch of sea salt
Pinch of caster sugar
1 tablespoon fresh lemon juice or lemon dressing

- Heat a dry wok or large frying pan over a medium heat, add the cashews and toast for 2–3 minutes until golden. Remove from the heat and leave to cool briefly, then finely chop the cashews and set aside.

- Put the grated carrots, sliced green chilli and chopped fresh coriander in a bowl. Add the toasted cashews, mix well and set aside.

- Heat the oil in a small pan over a medium heat. When the oil begins to shimmer, switch off the heat (the oil should be about 120°C/250°F). Add the cumin seeds, turmeric, sea salt and sugar, mix well, then immediately pour over the prepared salad.

- Toss the salad thoroughly to evenly coat everything in the spiced oil. Finish with the fresh lemon juice or lemon dressing, mix once more, cover and set aside in the refrigerator until needed. Serve cold.

CORIANDER CHUTNEY
(TRADITIONAL INDIAN STYLE)

Serves 4

This slightly spicy green chutney is perfect served with Chicken 65 (page 31) and is an essential part of Vada Pav (page 145).

1 large handful fresh coriander leaves (about 70g), larger/ thicker stems removed
1 fresh green finger chilli, deseeded
½ red onion, roughly chopped
2 garlic cloves, roughly chopped
¼ teaspoon chaat masala
Pinch of cumin powder
Pinch of caster sugar
50ml water
1 tablespoon fresh lemon juice or lemon dressing

- Put the fresh coriander leaves, green chilli, red onion, garlic, chaat masala, cumin powder, caster sugar, water and fresh lemon juice or lemon dressing in a blender and blend until smooth. Alternatively, use a pestle and mortar and pound the ingredients until the chutney is as smooth as you desire.

- The prepared chutney will keep well in a sealed container in the refrigerator for up to 2 days.

Variation
Add a little natural yogurt to the chutney for a smoother, creamier result.

DRY GARLIC COCONUT CHUTNEY
(TRADITIONAL INDIAN STYLE)

This dry chutney is an excellent addition to sandwiches of all kinds, and goes particularly well served alongside Disco Fry Egg (page 148).

Serves 4

4 tablespoons desiccated coconut
1 teaspoon Garlic Ginger Paste (page 228)
¼ teaspoon Kashmiri red chilli powder
Pinch of sea salt

- Heat a curry pan or frying pan without any oil over a low heat. Add the desiccated coconut and dry-fry for 2–3 minutes, or until the coconut begins to change colour slightly.

- Put the garlic ginger paste, red chilli powder and sea salt in a bowl. Add the dry-fried desiccated coconut and mix thoroughly. Set aside in the refrigerator for at least 1 hour before serving. The prepared chutney will keep well in the refrigerator for up to 3 days.

MINT CHUTNEY (TRADITIONAL INDIAN STYLE)

This recipe is packed full of flavour and is a good one for making ahead.

Serves 4–6

20g fresh mint leaves
1 small handful fresh coriander leaves (about 5g)
½ small red onion, finely chopped
¼–½ fresh green finger chilli, finely chopped
Pinch of sea salt
½ teaspoon caster sugar
¼ teaspoon Garlic Ginger Paste (page 228)
Dash of fresh lemon juice or lemon dressing
1–2 tablespoons water

- Put the mint leaves, coriander leaves, red onion, green chilli, sea salt and sugar in a pestle and mortar and grind until almost smooth. Add the garlic ginger paste, fresh lemon juice or lemon dressing and water (you may not need it all) and mix thoroughly.

- Serve or use the chutney immediately, for example with instant dosas (page 150), or store in an airtight container in the refrigerator for up to 3 days.

Variations
Try adding natural yogurt to make a minted yogurt dip, or add desiccated coconut for sweetness.

CUCUMBER RAITA (INDIAN RESTAURANT STYLE)

The cooling effects of both the cucumber and the yogurt make this raita the perfect partner to particularly spicy curry dishes.

Serves 4

½ tomato
¼ cucumber, peeled, deseeded and chopped
1 spring onion, thinly sliced
120ml natural yogurt
¼ teaspoon cumin powder
¼ teaspoon coriander powder
¼ teaspoon sea salt
1 small handful fresh coriander leaves, finely chopped

- Put the tomato in a heatproof bowl, cover with boiling water and let sit for 30 seconds. Strain the hot water and rinse the tomato with cold water. The skin should easily peel away. Deseed the peeled tomato and roughly chop.

- Put the prepared tomato, cucumber, spring onion, natural yogurt, cumin powder, coriander powder, sea salt and fresh coriander in a bowl. Mix thoroughly.

- Transfer the raita to a container, cover and set aside in the refrigerator for 1–2 hours before serving with your favourite curry dishes. The raita will keep well in the refrigerator for up to 3 days.

DATE & TAMARIND CHUTNEY
(TRADITIONAL INDIAN STYLE)

This delicious chutney is sweet and sticky, and perfect with Cauliflower Pakoras (page 23) or Aloo Channa Chaat (page 165).

Serves 8–10

60g dried tamarind block
150ml water, boiled
75g soft pitted dates
100g soft dark brown sugar
450ml water
½ teaspoon cumin powder
½ teaspoon coriander powder
½ teaspoon Kashmiri red chilli powder
1 teaspoon sea salt

- Put the dry tamarind in a heatproof bowl and cover with the 150ml boiled water. Mix briefly and set aside for 30 minutes. Pour the tamarind and water through a sieve into a separate bowl, pressing the tamarind into the sieve and scraping the bottom of the sieve with a spoon to collect as much tamarind paste as possible. Set the tamarind paste aside.

- Put the soft pitted dates, dark brown sugar and water in a saucepan. Bring to the boil, reduce the heat to low and simmer for 1 hour. Transfer the mixture to a blender and blend until smooth, then return the mixture to the pan, add the cumin powder, coriander powder, red chilli powder and sea salt. Add the prepared tamarind paste.

- Bring the chutney back to the boil, reduce the heat to medium and simmer for 25–30 minutes, or until it is slightly thick and syrupy. Set aside to cool completely, then pour into a container, seal with a lid and set aside in the refrigerator. The date and tamarind chutney will keep well in the refrigerator for up to 2 weeks.

RED CHILLI SAUCE (INDIAN RESTAURANT STYLE)

Serves 8

This spicy chilli sauce is perfect served alongside Vegetable Pakoras (page 18), Chicken Kebab (page 50) or as a dipping sauce for Poppadoms (page 215).

200ml tomato ketchup
1 teaspoon mint sauce
1 salad tomato, quartered
1 small onion, roughly chopped
½ small red pepper, roughly chopped
Pinch of cumin powder
Pinch of garam masala
½ teaspoon Kashmiri red chilli powder
½ teaspoon sea salt
Pinch of caster sugar
5 tablespoons tinned mixed fruit cocktail in natural juice
100ml water

- Put the tomato ketchup, mint sauce, salad tomato, onion, red pepper, cumin powder, garam masala, red chilli powder, sea salt, sugar, tinned fruit cocktail and water in a blender. Blend thoroughly until smooth.

- Pour the red chilli sauce into an airtight container and set aside in the refrigerator for 2 hours before use (or for up to 3 days).

211

PINK PAKORA SAUCE (INDIAN RESTAURANT STYLE)

You can easily double the ingredients (or scale it up further) to make a larger amount of pakora sauce as required.

Serves 3 (Makes 3 takeaway-sized tubs)

100ml tomato ketchup
50ml natural yogurt
½ teaspoon mint sauce
Pinch of cumin powder
½ teaspoon mild red chilli powder
Pinch of beetroot powder (optional, for colour)
Pinch of sea salt
Pinch of caster sugar
2–3 tablespoons water
50–75ml whole milk

- Put the tomato ketchup, natural yogurt, mint sauce, cumin powder, mild red chilli powder, beetroot powder (if desired), sea salt and caster sugar in a bowl. Mix well. Slowly add the water and then the milk, mixing well until the sauce reaches the desired consistency. Allow the sauce to stand for 5 minutes then mix once more. Pour the pakora sauce into an airtight container and set aside in the refrigerator for at least 1 hour before use. Serve with your favourite pakoras.

- The pink pakora sauce will keep well in the refrigerator for up to 2 days.

GARLIC SAUCE (INDIAN RESTAURANT STYLE)

Serves 1

4 tablespoons mayonnaise
½ teaspoon mild yellow mustard
¼ teaspoon garlic powder
Pinch of dried parsley
2–3 tablespoons whole milk

- Put the mayonnaise, yellow mustard, garlic powder and dried parsley in a bowl. Mix well. Slowly add the milk, mixing well until the sauce reaches the desired consistency. Set aside for 5 minutes, then mix once more and pour into a container. Seal and set aside in the refrigerator for 30 minutes before serving with Masala Fries (page 160).

- The prepared garlic sauce will keep well in an airtight container in the refrigerator for up to 2 days.

MINT SAUCE (INDIAN RESTAURANT STYLE)

This sauce is useful for cooling the palate between mouthfuls of particularly spicy curry dishes, or can be served as a starter alongside Spiced Onions (page 197) and Poppadoms (page 215).

Serves 1

4 tablespoons natural yogurt
½ teaspoon mint sauce
¼ teaspoon caster sugar
Pinch of turmeric
1 small handful fresh coriander leaves, finely chopped

- Put the natural yogurt, mint sauce, caster sugar, turmeric and fresh coriander in a bowl. Mix thoroughly, set aside for 5 minutes then mix once more. Pour the sauce into a container and set aside in the refrigerator for 1 hour before use. Serve alongside your favourite spicy curry dishes.

- The prepared mint sauce will keep well in an airtight container in the refrigerator for up to 2 days.

POPPADOMS (INDIAN RESTAURANT STYLE)

Readymade poppadoms are widely available but are often crunchy as opposed to light and crispy. I prefer to buy uncooked poppadoms and fry them myself as needed. Poppadoms need a very high heat to fry quickly, otherwise the oil can become clouded and isn't suitable for using again. If you don't want to waste too much oil, simply fill a pot or frying pan with a smaller amount of oil and break the uncooked poppadoms into smaller pieces before frying. The cooked poppadoms will keep well in an airtight container for up to 2 days.

Makes 8–10 poppadoms

Vegetable oil for deep-frying
1 pack of uncooked poppadoms (typically 8–10 per pack)

- Heat the oil for deep-frying to about 190°C/375°F. Carefully place an uncooked poppadom in the oil and press it down with a pair of tongs to ensure the poppadom is completely covered in oil. The poppadom will immediately puff up. Remove the cooked poppadom from the oil and set aside on a plate lined with kitchen paper to drain off any excess oil. Repeat the process until all of the poppadoms are fried.

- Serve the poppadoms with Spiced Onions (page 197), Mint Sauce (page 214) or alongside your favourite curry dishes.

MASALA POPPADOMS (INDIAN STREET-FOOD STYLE)

Serves 3 (Makes 6 poppadoms)

½ teaspoon chaat masala
Pinch of cumin powder
Pinch of Kashmiri red chilli powder
Pinch of sea salt
Pinch of ground black pepper
1 red onion, finely chopped
1 tablespoon fresh lemon juice or lemon dressing
2 salad tomatoes, deseeded and finely chopped
1 fresh green finger chilli, thinly sliced (deseeded if a
    milder spice level is preferred)
6 uncooked poppadoms
1 small handful fresh coriander leaves, finely chopped, to
    serve

- Put the chaat masala, cumin powder, red chilli powder, sea salt and black pepper in a small bowl. Mix and set aside.

- Put the red onion and fresh lemon juice or lemon dressing in a bowl, mix briefly and set aside for 5 minutes. Add the chopped tomatoes, fresh green chilli and prepared spices. Mix well.

- Fry the poppadoms (page 215) and place them on a serving plate. Dress each poppadom with the prepared spiced salad, top with fresh coriander and serve. Alternatively, break the poppadoms into smaller pieces and serve with the spiced salad on the side (Indian chips and dip!).

DRINKS AND DESSERTS

With an array of spices and full-on flavours across a huge variety of Indian dishes, choosing the right drink to accompany your meal is all-important. While many rookies will make the mistake of reaching for a glass of water to douse the heat of a spicy meal, real curry experts know that this simply cleanses the palate, leaving your mouth even more open to the numbing sensation of spice. Instead, opt for milk or yogurt-based drinks with a touch of sweetness. This chapter includes various lassi recipes, real refreshment to help you feel cool as a cucumber and ready to carry on eating!

Of course, the perfect way to finish any meal is with a sweet treat, and they don't come much sweeter than gulab jamun!

LASSI (INDIAN RESTAURANT STYLE)

This simple lassi recipe is the perfect way to cool down after indulging in a hot curry dish.

Serves 1

125ml natural yogurt
50ml whole milk
2 tablespoons cold water
2 teaspoons caster sugar
Seeds from 1 crushed green cardamom pod
Pinch of sea salt
2–3 ice cubes
2–3 shelled and finely chopped pistachios, to serve
   (optional)

- Put the natural yogurt, whole milk, cold water, caster sugar, seeds from the green cardamom pod, sea salt and ice cubes in a blender. Blend thoroughly for 30–40 seconds until the lassi is smooth.

- Pour into a tall serving glass, garnish with chopped pistachios (if desired) and serve.

STRAWBERRY LASSI (INDIAN RESTAURANT STYLE)

Serves 1

100g frozen strawberries
100ml natural yogurt
100ml whole milk
1 teaspoon caster sugar
Seeds from 1 crushed green cardamom pod
Pinch of sea salt
2–3 ice cubes
2–3 shelled and finely chopped pistachios, to serve
  (optional)

- Put the frozen strawberries, yogurt, whole milk, caster sugar, seeds from the green cardamom pod, sea salt and ice cubes in a blender. Blend thoroughly for 30–40 seconds until the lassi is smooth.

- Pour into a tall serving glass, garnish with chopped pistachios (if desired) and serve.

MANGO LASSI (INDIAN RESTAURANT STYLE)

Serves 1

1 large fresh, ripe mango, peeled, stone removed and
   pulp roughly chopped
100g natural yogurt
100ml whole milk
1–2 teaspoons caster sugar
Seeds from 1 crushed green cardamom pod
Pinch of sea salt
2–3 ice cubes
2–3 shelled and finely chopped pistachios, to serve
   (optional)

- Put the mango pulp, natural yogurt, whole milk, caster
  sugar (to taste), seeds from the green cardamom pod, sea
  salt and ice cubes in a blender. Blend thoroughly for 30–40
  seconds until the lassi is smooth.

- Pour into a tall serving glass, garnish with finely chopped
  pistachios (if desired) and serve.

MASALA CHAI, SPICED TEA
(TRADITIONAL INDIAN STYLE)

This spiced tea can be made ahead of time by preparing the brewed tea with the spices and allowing it to cool completely before storing in the refrigerator for up to 2 days. Finish with milk and sugar, as described, when desired.

Serves 1–2 (Makes about 250ml)

6 green cardamom pods
2 cloves
4 whole black peppercorns
½ cinnamon stick or cassia bark
3–4 thin slices fresh ginger
250ml water
2 black tea bags (or 2 teaspoons loose-leaf tea), to taste
125ml whole milk
2–3 teaspoons caster sugar, to taste

- Put the green cardamom pods, cloves, black peppercorns, cinnamon and fresh ginger slices in a pestle and mortar. Pound the whole spices and the ginger 3–4 times, just enough to lightly crush them and encourage the oils to be released from the spices.

- Tip the crushed spices into a saucepan, place it over a medium heat and dry-fry the spices for 1–2 minutes. Add the water, bring to the boil, then reduce the heat to low and simmer for 10 minutes. Add the tea bags or loose-leaf tea, remove from the heat and set aside to brew for 5 minutes. Strain the liquid through a fine sieve. At this stage the liquid can be cooled and set aside in the refrigerator for up to 2 days (if desired).

- To finish the tea, pour the spiced liquid into a pan. Add the milk and sugar, bring to the boil over a high heat, reduce the heat to low and simmer for 5 minutes. Pour the masala chai into a heatproof glass cup and serve.

GOLDEN MILK (TRADITIONAL INDIAN STYLE)

Also known as 'turmeric milk', this spiced drink is soothing and relaxing. A little fresh ginger can be used instead of ground ginger if desired.

Serves 1–2 (Makes 250ml)

  2 green cardamom pods
  1 teaspoon turmeric
  ½ teaspoon cinnamon powder
  ¼ teaspoon ground ginger
  2–3 black peppercorns
  1 teaspoon caster sugar
  250ml whole milk

- Crush the green cardamom pods with the back of a large knife. Put the crushed green cardamom in a bowl and add the turmeric, cinnamon powder, ground ginger, black peppercorns and sugar. Mix and set aside.

- Heat the milk in a saucepan over a medium heat and add the prepared spices. Bring to the boil, reduce the heat to medium-low and simmer for 5–6 minutes, stirring occasionally.

- Pour the golden milk through a fine sieve and serve.

GULAB JAMUN (INDIAN RESTAURANT STYLE)

Serves 3 (Makes 9)

175ml water
1 tablespoon rose water
1 green cardamom pod, crushed
100g caster sugar
Dash of fresh lemon juice or lemon dressing
60g milk powder
2 generous tablespoons plain flour
¼ teaspoon bicarbonate of soda
1 tablespoon ghee, melted
3–4 tablespoons whole milk
Vegetable oil for deep-frying
2–3 pistachios, shelled and finely chopped, to serve

- Put the water, rose water, crushed green cardamom pod, sugar and fresh lemon juice or lemon dressing in a saucepan. Stir the mix over a medium heat for 8–10 minutes until the mix slightly thickens and takes on a syrup-like texture. Remove from the heat and set aside.

- Put the milk powder, plain flour, bicarbonate of soda and melted ghee in a bowl. Mix and add just enough milk to bring the mixture together. Work the mixture only as much as necessary to form a dough.

- Oil your hands and form 9 smooth balls from the mix.

- Heat the oil for deep-frying to about 150°C/300°F. Carefully drop the prepared balls into the hot oil and fry for 4–5 minutes, or until the balls begin to float and are golden brown. Use a slotted spoon to remove the balls from the oil, place on a plate lined with kitchen paper to drain off any excess oil then set aside for 5 minutes.

- Place the balls into the prepared syrup mixture (if your syrup has cooled considerably, warm it up again for 1–2 minutes). Set aside for 1–2 hours until the syrup is absorbed fully by the balls. The gulab jamun can be prepared ahead and served cold, at room temperature, or warmed slightly in a pan with a little of the prepared syrup. When ready to serve, remove the gulab jamun from the syrup and arrange in serving bowls.

- Garnish the gulab jamun with the finely chopped pistachios and serve.

KULFI (TRADITIONAL INDIAN STYLE)

Sweet and cooling kulfi is the ultimate palate cleanser after a spicy meal.

Makes about 2.5 litres

550g mango pulp (from a tin)
225ml double cream
397g tin condensed milk
675ml whole milk
1 teaspoon ground almonds
Seeds from 6 crushed green cardamom pods

To serve (optional)
Shelled and peeled pistachios, finely chopped
Rose water

- Put the mango pulp, double cream, condensed milk, whole milk, ground almonds and cardamom seeds in a large bowl. Blend thoroughly with a stick blender until smooth.

- Pour the mango kulfi mix into ice-cream lolly moulds, kulfi moulds or a large freezer-safe container. Freeze for at least 8 hours, or overnight.

- To serve, arrange 1–2 scoops of kulfi per serving in a bowl and garnish with finely chopped pistachios and a splash of rose water (if desired).

MAKE YOUR OWN INGREDIENTS

Many readymade products are widely available nowadays (and are often very good), but it can be fun to make your own fresh batches of tasty ingredients for use in your Indian dishes, and if you enjoy cooking and preparing meals from scratch, making your own ingredients will probably be on your to-do list. It will often save you money, too.

Should you be planning to cook up a feast of curry dishes or simply want to get ahead, making your own batch of fresh garlic ginger paste is always a good idea. If it won't all be used in good time, you can portion it up in ice cube trays, ready to defrost quickly when required. Making your own tamarind and tandoori pastes ensures the maximum flavour in your dishes, too.

GARLIC GINGER PASTE

Indian restaurants typically prepare large quantities of garlic ginger paste for convenience. If you'd like to plan ahead for various dishes, it's handy to make the garlic ginger paste in bulk as described below. That being said, if you haven't prepared the paste, you can simply finely chop the required amount of fresh garlic and ginger, as indicated in each recipe. If time is short or you want to make life easier, shop-bought garlic ginger paste is more than acceptable; however, try to find a product without too many added flavours (especially vinegar-based pastes) as this may affect the flavour of dishes.

Makes 3–4 tablespoons garlic ginger paste (enough for 10–12 curry dishes)

6 large garlic cloves (about 30g peeled weight), roughly
  chopped
Similar quantity of fresh ginger (30g peeled weight),
  roughly chopped
1 tablespoon vegetable oil, plus extra for storing

- Put the chopped garlic, chopped ginger and vegetable oil in a blender and blend to a smooth paste – if necessary, add a touch of water to help bring everything together. Alternatively, use a pestle and mortar to make the garlic ginger paste by hand.

- Pour the blended garlic ginger paste into a container, add a touch more oil to help preserve its freshness, cover and set aside in the refrigerator for up to 5 days, or freeze in ice cube trays for future use.

Note

If a recipe calls for garlic ginger paste and you don't have any prepared, finely chop 1–2 fresh garlic cloves and grate a 2.5cm piece of fresh ginger and proceed as per the recipe.

TANDOORI PASTE

This paste is an essential ingredient in Chicken Pakoras (page 27) and Tandoori Chicken (pages 48 and 50), as well as various other dishes.

Makes about 50ml paste

1 teaspoon freshly grated ginger
1 teaspoon cumin powder
1 teaspoon coriander powder
½ teaspoon hot curry powder
½ teaspoon Kashmiri red chilli powder
¼ teaspoon paprika
Pinch of turmeric
Pinch of garlic powder
1 teaspoon dried fenugreek leaves (methi)
¼ teaspoon sea salt
¼ teaspoon mint sauce
½ teaspoon Tamarind Paste (page 232)
1 tablespoon vegetable oil
2 tablespoons water

- Put the grated ginger, cumin powder, coriander powder, hot curry powder, red chilli powder, paprika, turmeric, garlic powder, dried fenugreek leaves, sea salt, mint sauce, tamarind paste, vegetable oil and water in a bowl. Mix thoroughly and set aside for 5 minutes.

- Mix thoroughly once again, transfer to an airtight container and set aside in the refrigerator until needed. The paste will keep well for up to 3 days.

TAMARIND PASTE

Tamarind paste can be used to add a slightly sour tang to your favourite curry dishes (try it in vindaloo) and is an essential ingredient in homemade Tandoori Paste (page 230).

Makes about 3 tablespoons of tamarind paste

25g dried tamarind block
50ml boiling water

- Put the dried tamarind block in a heatproof bowl. Cover with boiling water, mix briefly and set aside for 30 minutes.

- Pour the tamarind and water through a sieve into a separate bowl. Press the tamarind block into the sieve to extract as much of the tamarind as possible, scraping the bottom of the sieve to collect the paste.

- Transfer the tamarind paste to a container, cover and set aside in the refrigerator until needed for use in recipes. The tamarind paste will keep well for up to 3 days.

PANEER CHEESE

If you've never tried making your own cheese, this is a great place to start. Paneer is perhaps the easiest of all cheeses to make fresh, and the end result makes the process very worthwhile!

Makes about 200g

1 litre whole milk
3 tablespoons distilled vinegar mixed with 2 tablespoons
   water
Sea salt, to taste

- Put the milk in a large saucepan and heat over a medium heat until it's just about to boil, stirring occasionally. Add the vinegar and water mix and use a spatula to stir it gently into the milk. The milk should begin to curdle, and the curds and whey will separate. Set the pan aside and leave it to sit for 15 minutes.

- Line a sieve with clean muslin or a cheesecloth, place it over a large bowl and pour the mix through the sieve. Squeeze the mix tightly through the cheesecloth to remove all of the liquid. Open up the cheesecloth again and season the cheese with a little sea salt. Squeeze once more and tie the cheese tightly in the cloth. Put the prepared paneer cheese on a plate and weight it down with something heavy (a large tin of beans or similar will suffice). Set the weighed-down paneer cheese aside in the refrigerator for 1 hour to set.

- Once the cheese is set, remove it from the cheesecloth, cover tightly with cling film and refrigerate until ready to use (up to 2 days).

- Use your homemade paneer as desired, or dice it into small cubes and stir-fry in a little oil for 2–3 minutes before adding it to your favourite curry dishes.

INDEX

235